SOPRINTENDENZA ARCHEOLOGICA DI ROMA

THE ROMAN FORUM

D1396899

ELECTA

THE MONUMENTAL DEVELOPMENT OF THE FORUM

"This ground, where now are the forums, was once occupied by wet swamps: a ditch was drenched with the water that overflowed from the river. The Lake of Curtius, which supports dry altars, is now solid ground, but formerly it was a lake. Where now the processions are wont to defile through the Velabrum to the Circus, there was nought but willows and hollows canes."
(Ovid, *Fasti* VI, 401-406)

As the words of Ovid reveal, Roman tradition retained a clear memory of the original marshy character of the Forum, a valley positioned between the Capitol to the north-west, and the Palatine to the south-east. The Forum was traversed by one of the many streams that flowed into the Tiber, the Velabrum, which rendered the plain unhealthy. Since its marshy character made it unsuitable for human habitation, the plain was used between the X and IX centuries B.C. as a sepulchral area connected to one of the inhabited sites on the hills surrounding the valley (the Palatine, the Velia, the Capitol). The unification of these hilltop sites in the first half of the VIII century B.C. determined the form of the city of Rome. The traditional date of the foundation of the city (754/753 B.C.) almost exactly coincides with the unification of the villages, demonstrable on archaeological grounds by the abandonment of separate sepulchral areas and the creation of the large communal necropolis on the Esquiline. The cemetery in the Forum

came to be restricted to the burial of non-adult members of the community, those who could be buried even within the city, until, towards the end of the VII century B.C., even this usage ceased.

The first essential step towards the permanent occupation of the Forum valley was the channelling of the Velabrum, achieved through the construction of the Cloaca Maxima, a grandiose work traditionally ascribed to the first king of the Etruscan dynasty, Tarquinius Priscus. Again the correspondence between the data provided by the literary sources and those retrievable from the archaeological evidence is almost perfect, since the Forum's earliest pavement of beaten earth is dated to just around 600 B.C. From this period onwards, the Forum, became the centre of civic life and was progressively occupied by buildings connected with political, religious and mercantile activities, but also by honorific statues and other commemorative monuments, everlasting symbols of the important military and political exploits of Roman history that contributed to the development of the Forum as the place par excellence of the collective memory.

At the two far ends of the large open square, almost at the same time, the *Regia*, that is, the residence of the king, and the first Comitium were built. Very few vestiges of the Comitium, the earliest centre of political activity of the city created by the unification under Romulus, have

*1. General view
of the Roman Forum
from the Capitol*

survived the modifications of the Caesarean and Augustan periods. Stratigraphic excavations of the Comitium area, in the north corner of the Forum at the foot of the *Arx* of the Capitol, have ascertained the existence of eight superimposed levels that correspond to as many pavings and chronological phases. Contemporary with the second paving of the Comitium, datable around 570 B.C. and therefore at the height of the Regal period, is an Archaic monumental complex, now closed to visitors, consisting of an altar with three wings, a column base, and a cippus bearing sacred laws inscribed in Archaic Latin. It is the *Niger Lapis*, regarded as a sanctuary of Vulcan of great antiquity, near which Romulus disappeared, thereby rendering it a tragic place. The site was distinguished, from the Sullan period onwards, by a section of black marble pavement delimited by a fence (whence the name *Niger Lapis*) which was respected by subsequent pavings of the Comitium. In contrast, the *Regia* was built in the area behind the remains of the Temple of Divus Julius. Under the building now visible, whose original plan perhaps dates to the last years of the Etruscan monarchy (around 525 B.C.), it has been possible to see the remains of a series of successive buildings constructed between the VIII and the mid VI century B.C. A group of huts were in fact demolished in order to make room for a building of larger dimensions; scarce evidence of successive restorations to this building survives. Thanks to the discovery of a fragment of Bucchero ware of the VI century B.C. inscribed with the word *rex*, it has been possible to identify, with absolute certainty, this building with the *Regia*, the construction of which is ascribed to the king Numa Pompilius by literary sources. The private homes of some of his successors were later added to the residence of the second king of Rome, continuing to the east along the

via Sacra. But it seems that the primitive king's home represents only part of a much larger architectural complex, that also included the House of the Vestals and that of the *rex sacrorum* (who in the Republican period assumed some of the religious duties of the king). This complex is paralleled by the plans and functions of the Etruscan palaces known for example at Murlo (Siena) and at Acquarossa (Viterbo), where the residential areas are closely associated with sites reserved for worship.

After the expulsion of the kings (509 B.C.), particular attention was given to the construction of buildings strictly connected with the events and the new institutions of the newly created Republic: the so-called Rostra, the tribune from which the magistrates spoke, that assumed this name only after 338 B.C. when the rostra from the ships from Antium were fixed to it; the Temple of Saturn, provided with a large forecourt that functioned as the seat of the Aerarium, the state Treasury; the Temple of the Castores, dedicated to the divine twins, Castor and Pollux, whose appearance propitiated the Roman victory at Lake Regillus (499 B.C.) over the Latin League that was supporting Tarquinius Superbus in his attempt to reconquer the city.

From the end of the IV century B.C. onwards, the open area of the Roman Forum began to be populated by bronze honorific statues, like those of Lucius Furius Camillus and of Gaius Menius, who defeated the Latin League at Antium in 338 B.C., or by columns such as the one of the same Gaius Menius; all of these monuments celebrated individual military glory. Around the middle of the II century B.C., the presence of honorific statues of former magistrates had become so invasive that the censors of 158 B.C., Publius Cornelius Scipio and Marcus Popilius, had them all removed, except those voted directly by the senate and

2. Archaic sanctuary under the Niger Lapis: detail of the base and the cippus with an Archaic Latin inscription

3. Plan of the Forum in the Republican period

the Roman people (Pliny, *Natural History*, XXXIV, 30). The commemorative sculptures, that in the mid-Republican period adorned the Forum square but unfortunately have not survived, did not neglect even the great plebeian political victories. In 294 B.C., Quintus Marcius Censorinus, the first plebeian to become censor, erected a statue of Marsyas in the Forum area (copies of this statue are known from the Latin colonies of *Paestum* and *Alba Fucens*). The statue represents the Silenus, with his feet still tight in the bonds but represented in a liberating movement, a clear allusion to the abolition of slavery due to debts, an important plebeian conquest of the last years of the IV century B.C.

During the III century B.C. the building operation of greatest relevance which took place in the Forum area was the construction of the *Macellum* to the north of the square, in the same place where a few centuries later (A.D. 71-75) the Emperor Vespasian built the *Templum Pacis*, the grandiose monumental square, built to commemorate the victory over the Jews and that perhaps retained, at least in part, the form of the Republican market which it replaced.

The construction of a building dedicated to the development of activities linked with retail commerce in a secluded site and the progressive replacement of the butcher's shops with shops for money changers, marked an irreversible change in the conception of the Forum space and translated into concrete form the principal requirement contained in the notion of *forensis dignitas* ('dignity of the Forum') expressed by Varro.

A further development in the rationalisation of the functions and spaces of the Forum was achieved in the course of the II century B.C. with the construction of the civic basilicas, thereby introducing a new building type, destined to become one of the most characteristic and representative elements of the urban landscape in the Roman world, whereas the building works of the Sullan period, chiefly located in the area of the Curia and on the Capitol, enriched the west side of the Forum square with an extraordinary architectonic backdrop: the splendid facade of the *Tabularium*, the building destined to contain the

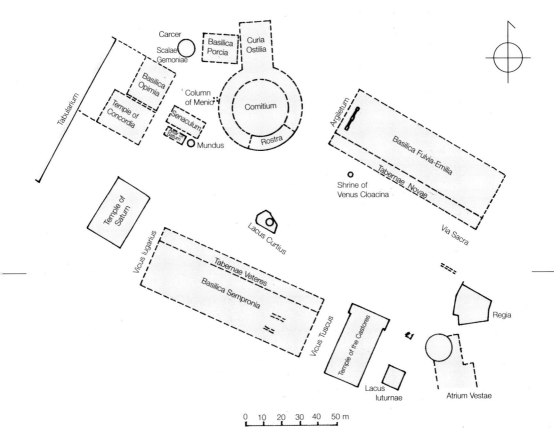

0 10 20 30 40 50 m

public archives of the State. In the Caesarean period, the old Republican square underwent radical changes in the Comitium area with the demolition of the Sullan Curia Hostilia and the construction of the Curia Julia. The Curia Julia, completed by Augustus, was erected as a kind of monumental appendix to the new Forum that the dictator had built extending from the west corner of the Basilica Fulvia-Aemilia in the direction of the Capitol. The Forum of Caesar initiated a succession of monumental squares annexed to the Republican Forum to celebrate the glory of the Imperial families.

Augustus' building activity in the Roman Forum transformed the short east side of the Republican square into a space devoted to the glorification of the Julian family, significantly counter-poised to the short west side with the Curia, the earlier Rostra, and the Temple of Saturn, symbols of the Republican tradition against which the Augustan regime set itself as the providential consequence. In front of the Temple of Divus Julius, dedicated to the deified founder of the dynasty, a new orators' tribune was therefore built, the *Rostra ad Divi Iulii*, adorned with the rostra from the ships of Antonius and Cleopatra seized at Actium in 31 B.C., whereas the temple was flanked, on the north and south, by two arches that commemorated respectively Augustus' victory over Antonius at Actium, and the victory over the Parthians. The Parthian arch was evocatively connected to the Portico that bordered the south side of the Basilica Fulvia-Aemilia, that was dedicated to Gaius and Lucius Caesar, the nephews and adoptive sons of the Prince, his designated heirs in the succession.

The political building projects of successive Imperial dynasties added prestigious elements to the Forum area, that following the projects of the Augustan period had assumed the appearance of an authentic monumental square. It was in the tradition established by Augustus with the construction of the Temple of Divus Iulius that the Temple of Vespasian and Titus and the Temple dedicated by Antoninus Pius to his wife Faustina, who died and was deified in A.D. 141, and which was dedicated to the Emperor as well posthumously, were built. On the west end of the square, the point at which the via Sacra divides to join the two hills of the Capitol came to be occupied, at the beginning of the III century A.D., by the monumental Arch of Septimius Severus; this arch celebrated the emperor's victories over the Parthians and, not by chance, was positioned opposite the Parthian Arch of Augustus, that commemorated the restitution to the Romans of the standards captured from Crassus' legions in the battle of Carrae (55 B.C.).

Following the damage caused by the Neronian fire of A.D. 64, that in this area was focused on the north slopes of the Palatine (the area now between the House of the Vestal Virgins and the Arch of Titus), numerous restorations were necessary after other devastating fires that one by one damaged many of the buildings of the Forum between the end of the II century A.D. and the late Antique period. The Temple of Vesta and the House of the Vestal Virgins were almost entirely rebuilt in A.D. 191. Many buildings in the west of the square (Curia Julia, Temple of Saturn, Basilica Julia) that were damaged by the fire of Carinus (A.D. 283) were rebuilt under Diocletian, whereas the damage caused anew in the Basilica Julia and the Basilica Fulvia-Aemilia by the sack of Alaric (A.D. 410) was repaired in the course of the

---

4. Denarius of Marcus Aemilius Lepidus depicting the Basilica Fulvia-Aemilia

5. Aureus of Octavianus depicting the Temple of Divus Julius

Work in the Forum from Romulus to Tarquinius Superbus according to tradition

Romulus (754/3-715 B.C.) One version of the ancient tradition ascribes the choice and exploitation of the Forum valley as the centre of the new city to the first king of Rome (and to the Sabine Titus Tatius, co-opted to the throne). Some of the most ancient sites in the area are connected with both, or with Romulus alone (Shrine of Venus Cloacina, *Lacus Curtius*, *Volcanal*, Temple of Jupiter Stator, Shrine of *Janus Geminus*).

Numa Pompilius (715-672 B.C.) In addition to the Temple of Vesta, the second king of Rome built the *Regia* and instituted the cult of the *Doliola*.

Tullus Hostilius (672-640 B.C.) He is said to have built the first Curia, the so-called Hostilia, and lived on the Velia.

first decade of the V century A.D.

The last systematic monumental project in the Forum and its immediate vicinity dates to the first years of the IV century A.D. and bears the mark of the Emperor Maxentius. This emperor, who re-established the capital in Rome, in clear contrast with the new centres of Imperial power chosen by the Tetrarchs (Nicomedia and Salonika for the Eastern part of the empire and Milan and Treviri for the Western one), wanted to revitalise its ancient political and religious heart, replete with the symbols of its thousand-year history. This explains the emperor's decision to erect the statue of Mars near the *Niger Lapis*, and to reconstruct the Temple of Jupiter Stator, built according to tradition at the point where the Latins led by Romulus repelled the assault of the Sabines led by Titus Tatius, and perhaps dedicated at the same time to the Emperor's son Romulus. But the building tied more than any other to the building activity of Maxentius is without doubt the impressive Basilica erected on the Velia, heavily restored at the end of the IV century A.D., which has been recognised as the headquarters of the civil praefect, a figure who in the late Antique period became fundamental for the administrative management of Rome.

The long history of the monuments of the Roman Forum ends with the large Column erected in A.D. 608 in honour of an obscure and bloodthirsty Byzantine emperor, Phocas, ditinguished in the eyes of the Roman Church for having donated to Pope Boniface IV the Pantheon, which was later transformed into a church named S. Maria *ad Martyres*.

From the abandonment to the rediscovery

Very little of the ancient splendour of the Forum was still visible to the unknown German pilgrim who, passing through Rome in the middle of the VIII century A.D., compiled a brief description of the city. From those traveller's notes, combined with others in a collection known as the Itinerarium Einsiedlense (or Anonymous of Einsiedeln) after the German monastery where it was preserved, it is clear that the buildings still identifiable in that period were those built on the slopes of the Capitol: the Arch of Septimius Severus, the Curia Julia, the Temples of Concord and of Vespasian (of which the dedicatory inscription was transcribed, later almost completely lost). Other monuments in contrast are difficult for us to identify, such as the large base of an equestrian statue of the Emperor Constantine (the *Equus Constantini*), seen within the square and today only hypothetically recognisable in a few remains of the foundation on which the Decennalia base was positioned. From the date of the latest monument erected in the Forum, the Column of Phocas, little more than two centuries had passed, yet by then abandonment and intentional destructions had transformed the Forum into a field of ruins, placed at any rate outside the Mediaeval city that was concentrated in the ancient quarter of the *Subura* or had begun to occupy the great public buildings of the Campus Martius. The only surviving monuments were the few temples transformed into churches from the VI century A.D. onwards: S. Adriano inside the Curia Julia, SS. Cosma e Damiano in the Temple of Romulus, S. Maria Antiqua in a building connected with the *Athenaeum* of Hadrian, the Oratory of the Forty Martyrs near the *Lacus Iuturnae*, to which was added, in the VIII century, the Church of S. Lorenzo in Miranda, built in the cella of the Temple of Antoninus and Faustina. A few other buildings were preserved instead because they were encased in fortified complexes that belonged to aristocratic families, the most

Ancus Marcius (640-616 B.C.) Traditionally identified as the builder of the first *Carcer* (prison); this building is now outside the excavations area of the Roman Forum.

Tarquinius Priscus (616-578 B.C.) He initiated the land reclamation in the Forum valley and erected the statue of the augur *Attus Navius* in the Comitium.

Servius Tullius (578-534 B.C.) Tradition attributes to him the construction of the earliest walls and of the most important monuments in the Forum Boarium and on the Aventine. In the Roman Forum, the sources record an enlargement of the *Carcer* and the creation of the *vicus Tuscus* that, following the course of the Velabrum, joined the Forum square with the Forum Boarium.

Tarquinius Superbus (534-509 B.C.) He completed the land reclamation in the Forum valley by building the Cloaca Maxima, and perhaps initiated the construction of the Temple of Saturn, which was dedicated only after the foundation of the Republic.

famous of which was the Frangipane family who used the Arch of Titus in this way. The abandonment of the site and the transformation of the temples into sites of Christian cult was responsible for the progressive obliteration of the Forum from the collective memory of the city and the few attempts to restore its ancient appearance, as for example contained in the *Mirabilia Urbis Romae*, the guide for the entire Middle Ages to the monuments of the city, confused irreparably the buildings and interwined legends of Christian and pagan origin into an indissoluble tangle. Nevertheless, during the Mediaeval period, in the area that had become nothing more than pasture land, such as to merit the name of Campo Vaccino, many buildings were still jealously preserved by the dirt which over time had accumulated higher and higher; the original ground level had become so deep that in the XII century the floor of the Church of S. Adriano had to be raised by about four metres to coincide with that of the roads around the church. But it was during the Renaissance that the Forum suffered the almost complete loss of many buildings; for the renovation of the city, Pope Julius II initiated on a large scale the exploitation of this area as a quarry, reusing the material, but more often reducing to lime, as much as could be recovered. The forum regained its ancient splendour for a single moment, when, in order to celebrate the entry of Charles V into Rome, after his victory over the Turks (1536), Pope Paul III created a temporary triumphal way from the Arch of Titus to the Arch of Septimius Severus, that served as the model for all other triumphal spectacles that were produced to celebrate kings, emperors and generals down to the end of the XVIII century. The most extensive destruction took place in the years between 1540 and 1550, as a direct consequence of the intensification of work for the construction of S. Pietro; the areas around the Temples of Saturn and of Vespasian, the Curia Julia, the Basilica Aemilia, the Temples of the Castores and of Divus

Julius and the entire road from the Temple of Antoninus and Faustina to the Arch of Titus was turned into a quarry. Particularly severe was the fate suffered by the Temple of Divus Julius, the Arches of Augustus flanking the temple, and the *Regia*; as recorded in the chronicles of this work written by contemporary eye-witnesses who were involved in various ways in the recuperation of material, such as Pirro Ligorio and Onofrio Panvinio, the destruction of these monuments, still in large part intact, occurred quickly, in some cases in the course of a single month. Futile were the proposals of Raphael to preserve the ancient Roman monuments or Michaelangelo's reservations concerning the robber excavations of those years. The new Rome that celebrated the glory of the Popes destroyed that of the Caesars in precisely the period in which the rediscovery of the past was revived in the refined and highly cultured Renaissance courts. In the XVI and XVII centuries, very little was still visible on the surface to justify new campaigns for the recuperation of material; the Forum was essentially abandoned, except for the row of elms that traversed it from the Arch of Titus to that Septimius Severus, under which reposed the shepherds who took their flocks there to graze. It was the new vision of the ancient world that sprung from the work of J. J. Winckelmann that marked a decisive change in the languishing studies of Roman archaeology. The preambles of modern archaeology thereafter saw the Forum as a privileged setting for study: the work led by Carlo Fea, a sensitive source of inspiration for the principles of the conservation of ancient monuments, constitutes the first steps of the long activity of excavation and research that has had as its protagonists, following the unification of Italy, Pietro Rosa, Giuseppe Fiorelli and above all Rodolfo Lanciani and Giacomo Boni. The results of their work are seen today by the visitors who everyday visit the Archaeological Area of the Roman Forum.

*6. Constant Moyaux
(1835-1911).
West side of the Forum,
reconstruction*

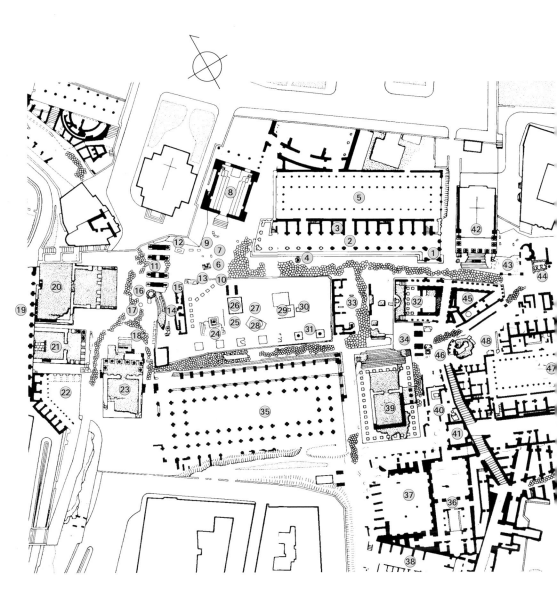

1. Large dedicatory inscription
2. Portico of Gaius and Lucius Caesar
3. *Tabernae Novae*
4. Shrine of Venus Cloacina
5. Basilica Fulvia-Aemilia
6. *Niger Lapis*
7. Comitium
8. Curia Julia
9. Base of the statue of Mars
10. Column base of Arcadius,
    Honorius and Theodosius
11. Arch of Septimius Severus
12. Base of Constantius II
13. Decennalia Base
14. Imperial Rostra
15. *Rostra Vandalica*
16. *Mundus/Umbilicus Urbis*
17. Altar of Saturn
18. *Miliarium Aureum*
19. *Tabularium*

20. Temple of Concord
21. Temple of Vespasian and Titus
22. Portico of the Dei Consentes
23. Temple of Saturn with the Aerarium
24. Column of Phocas
25. Inscription of *L. Naevius Surdinus*
26. *Ficus, olea, vitis*
27. Small well-heads
28. *Lacus Curtius*
29. *Doliola*

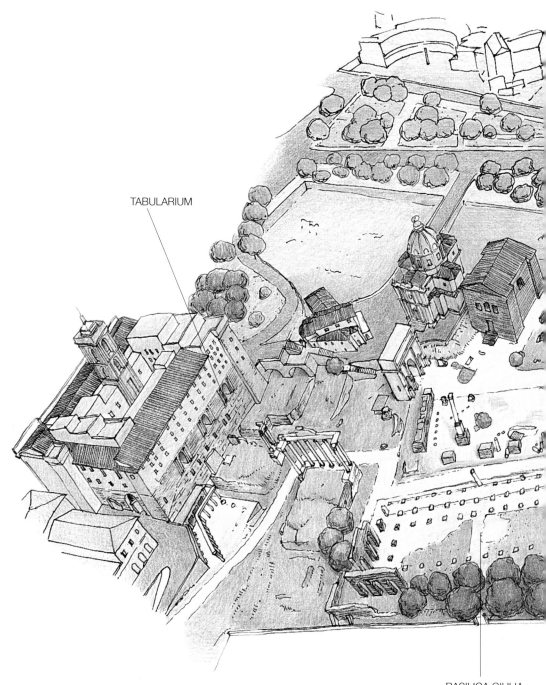

TABULARIUM

BASILICA GIULIA

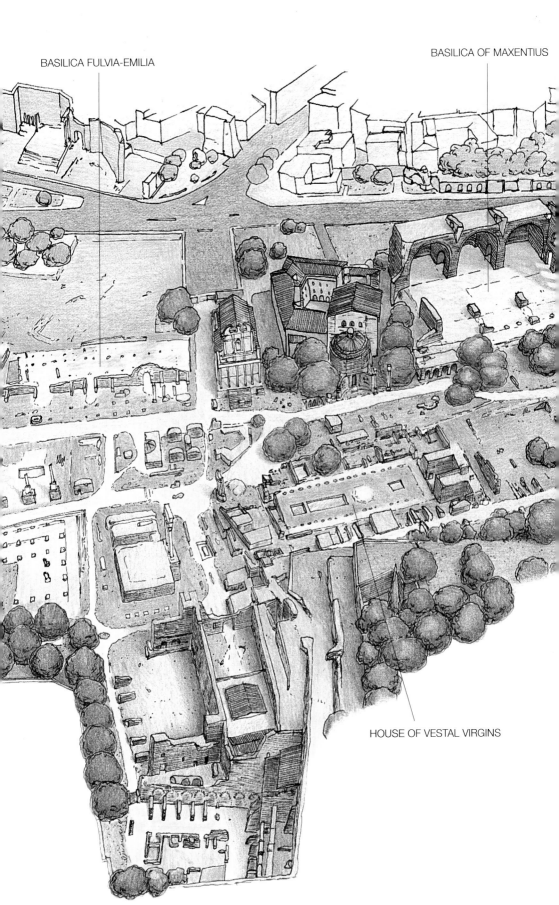

BASILICA FULVIA-EMILIA

BASILICA OF MAXENTIUS

HOUSE OF VESTAL VIRGINS

Chronology of the rediscovery of the Forum from 1870

1870
Beginning of work to isolate the Temple of the Castores, already excavated in part between 1811 and 1812.
1871
Completion of excavation of the Basilica Julia, to a large extent already brought to light between the end of the XVIII century and the mid XIX century.
1872
Discovery of the Plutei of Trajan in the central square of the Forum; the reliefs are now exhibited in the Curia Julia.
1872-1874
Excavation of the central square of the Forum and the definitive clearing of the Column of Phocas.
1876
Excavations along the facade of the Temple of Antoninus and Faustina; the lower part of the columns and the pronaos had already been cleared in the course of work between 1807 and 1811.
1877
Excavation of the via Sacra. Identification and excavation of the Temple of Vesta.
1878-1879
Excavation in the area of the *Horrea Vespasiani*, at that time identified with the *Porticus Margaritaria* (the warehouse of pearls).
1879-1883
Beginning of the excavations in the House of the Vestal Virgins.
1880
Excavation of the via Sacra. Clearing of the front of the Temple of Romulus.
1882
Excavation of the via Sacra. Discovery of the aedicula (small shrine) at the entrance to the House of the Vestal Virgins.
1886-1888
First excavations of the *Regia*.

1896-1898
Excavation in the area of the Temple of the Castores.
1898
Completion of work clearing the *clivus Capitolinus*, already partially excavated in 1810.
Beginning of excavations in the area of the Republican Comitium, identified by T. Mommsen in 1845.
Clearing of the facade of the Temple of Divus Julius. Conclusion of work near the *Regia*.
Restoration of the aedicula at the entrance to the House of the Vestal Virgins.
1899
Discovery of the base of the equestrian statue of Constantius II.
Identification of the *Niger Lapis*.
Beginning of excavations of the Basilica Fulvia-Aemilia and the *Tabernae Novae*. Test excavations by R. Lanciani under the Basilica of Maxentius, that revealed remains belonging to the *Horrea Piperataria*.
Dismantling of the Imperial phase of the via Sacra.
1900
Excavation of the facade of the Curia Julia. Stratigraphic test trenches by G. Boni in the area of the Republican Comitium. Discovery of the Shrine of Venus Cloacina. Demolition of the Church of S. Maria Liberatrice and continuation of the excavations in the House of the Vestal Virgins. Removal of the Imperial road at the level of the Arch of Titus.
1900-1901
Excavation of the Church of S. Maria Antiqua and of the Domitianic Buildings, at that time identified with the Temple of Augustus. Excavation of the *Lacus Iuturnae*.

1900-1904
Conclusion of the isolation of the Temple of the Castores.
1900-1910
Excavation worksite in the Basilica Fulvia-Aemilia.
1902
Excavation of the tunnels of the Caesarean period situated under the central square of the Forum. Discovery of the subterranean level of a private house along the via Sacra, considered to be part of a brothel. Excavation of the basins of the fountain in the centre of the peristyle of the House of the Vestal Virgins.
1902-1903
Excavation of the Iron Age cemetery near the Temple of Antoninus and Faustina.
1902-1904
Partial excavation of the *Horrea Agrippiana*.
1903
Discovery of the area of the *Doliola*, identified with the remains of the base of the *Equus Domitiani*. Test trenches in the area of the *Lacus Iuturnae*. Test trenches by G. Boni in the Basilica of Maxentius.
1904
Discovery of the *Lacus Curtius*. Recovery of the reliquary with ceramic material from the VII century B.C. from inside the *Doliola*.
Discovery (?) of the remains of the House of Marcus Aemilius Scaurus.
1908 (?)
Planting of laurels along the road between the Sacellum of Bacchus and the Basilica of Maxentius.
1911-1912
Excavation of the central courtyard of the *Horrea Agrippiana*.
1930
Beginning of work inside the Curia Julia to remove the decorative elements of the Baroque Church of S. Adriano.
1930-1932
Excavation of the north part of the Basilica Fulvia-Aemilia.

1936-1938
Resumption and conclusion of work in the Curia Julia.
1936-1939
Completion of the excavation of the Basilica Fulvia-Aemila, which brought to light the entire north side and the north-west corner.
1946-1948
Test trenches in the central nave and along the west side of the Basilica Fulvia-Aemilia, which brought to light remains of earlier building phases.
1953-1955
Reconstruction of the shrine of Juturna following the architect A. Davico's design.
1955
Restoration of the inscription of *L. Naevius Surdinus* in the square of the Forum.
1960
Stratigraphic test trenches inside the Basilica Julia, that resulted in the discovery of part of the earlier Basilica Sempronia and an earlier house, that probably belonged to Scipio Africanus.

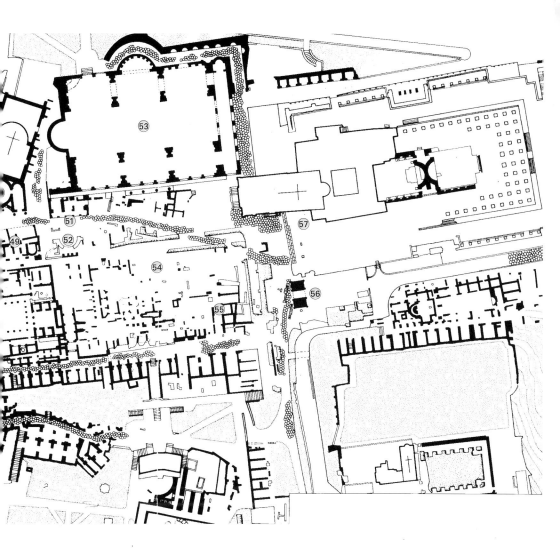

Suggestions for the Forum visit

The concentration within a relatively restricted space, such as the Forum, of buildings and monuments belonging to very different periods which often do not overlap, makes a visit which takes into account the chronological development of this area very difficult. You are advised instead to follow the topographical itineraries proposed, beginning the visit at the north end of the Forum square, that is, that towards the via dei Fori Imperiali, and going round in a counter-clockwise direction; having considered in detail the monuments facing onto the Forum, the visit continues in the direction of the Palatine to conclude at the Arch of Titus.

A view of the entire area open to the public can be seen from two evocative vantage points: the viewing point of the Forum from the Farnesina Gardens on the Palatine and the terraces outside the excavation area, along via di S. Pietro in Carcere, that leads up from via dei Fori Imperiali to the Capitol.

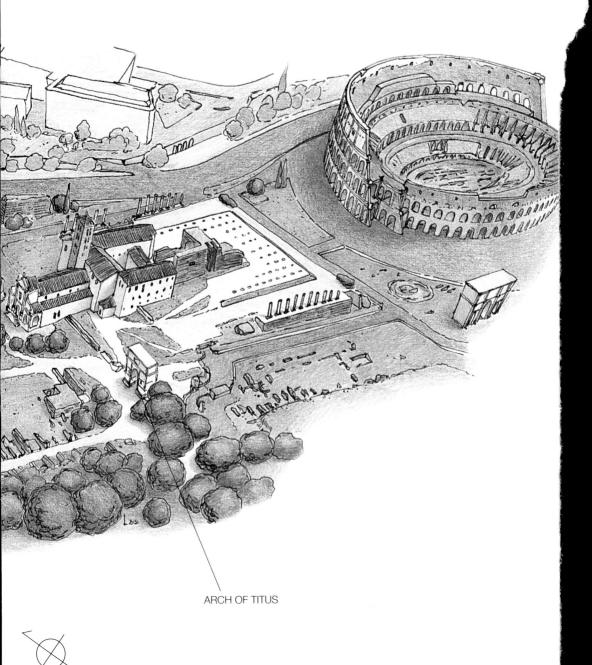

ARCH OF TITUS

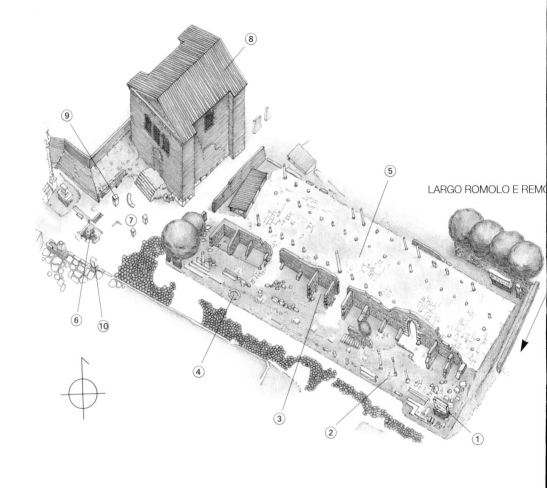

LARGO ROMOLO E REM

1. Large dedicatory inscription
2. Portico of Gaio and Lucio Cesari
3. *Tabernae Novae*
4. Shrine of Venus Cloacina
5. Basilica Fulvia-Emilia
6. *Niger Lapis*
7. Comitium
8. Curia Julia
9. Base of the statue of Mars
10. Column base of Arcadius, Honorius and Theodosius

THE NORTH SIDE OF THE FORUM:
FROM THE BASILICA FULVIA-AEMILIA TO THE CURIA JULIA

The entrance to the Archaeological Area of the Roman Forum is next to Largo Romolo e Remo. A modern ramp between the Temple of Antoninus and Faustina ㊷ and the Basilica Fulvia-Aemilia ⑤, provides access to the Forum level, along the west side of the via Sacra. The road at this point lacks its ancient basalt paving, that on the contrary is well-preserved proceeding in the direction of the Arch of Septimius Severus ⑪. The settlement of this pavement, brought to light by the excavations, dates to Augustus period.

Turning right at the end of this entrance ramp, we see a large **dedicatory inscription** ①, supported by four small piers of modern bricks, that records the dedication of the Senate in 2 B.C. to Lucius Caesar, the son of Augustus and grandson of the deified Caesar, as *Princeps Iuventutis* and consul designate. He was the son of Agrippa and Julia, the grandson and adoptive son of Augustus, who together with his brother Gaius was identified as a possible heir to the empire, before their untimely death opened the road to succession

to Tiberius. The inscription, now out of position, perhaps belonged to a large triple arch that crossed the via Sacra at this point. It has been recognised as the lost Parthian Arch of Augustus, dedicated to the emperor in 19 B.C., to commemorate

the restitution to the Romans of the standards captured by the Parthians from Crassus' legions in 55 B.C. after their defeat at Carrae. This event, more the result of shrewd diplomatic activity than of military exploits, became one of the central themes of

---

7. Shrine of Venus Cloacina at the time of excavation

The myths of the Forum: the Romano-Sabine war

The story of the Romano-Sabine war (among other sources, Plutarch, *Life of Romulus*, 18,1-9) established the foundation myths of many Archaic cults in the

Forum. After Titus Tatius' Sabines conquered the Capitol, Romulus challenged them to battle in the Forum valley, a rough and difficult terrain, where, moreover, a few days before the river had flooded, depositing deep and dangerous mud. One of the Sabine knights,

Curtius, ventured forward ahead of the rest of the army at the risk of being swallowed by the mud. From this episode, the site took the name of *Lacus Curtius*. Many other short clashes followed and Romulus himself, having been hit on the head by a stone,

Augustan propaganda to such an extent that it was reproduced on the relief that adorned the Emperor's cuirass on the statue discovered near the villa of Livia at Prima Porta. A bronze copy of this statue has been placed on the via dei Fori Imperiali where the remains of the Forum of Augustus are now visible. Proceeding along the Via Sacra, on the right stand the remains of a portico, of which three granite columns, dated to the V century A.D., have been re-erected. This arrangement was preceded by an earlier colonnade, as evidenced by a series of travertine column bases that belong to the **Portico of Gaius and Lucius Caesar** ② , built in this area during the last

decade of the I century B.C. Most probably some of the architectural elements that are now piled up along the entire length of the ancient colonnade are associated with the decoration of this Portico. Fragments of spiral decoration, some marble metopes decorated with bucrania and paterae, parts of coffered ceilings and gigantic Corinthian capitals are of particular interest. Immediately behind the Portico, some wall sections in opus quadrata of Aniene tuff are the only remains of a row of shops that opened along the entire south facade of the Basilica Fulvia-Aemilia, to which they belonged. Called the *Tabernae Novae* ③ , they have been rebuilt many times since their

original construction during the Republican period; money-changers (*argentarii*) carried out their activity in these shops and as a result, the shops also took the name of *Tabernae Argentariae*. Near the western part of the Portico of Gaius and Lucius Caesar, at the point corresponding to the place where the Cloaca Maxima entered the Forum, the presence of a marble enclosure that belonged to a small round building, identified with the **Sacellum of Venus Cloacina** ④ is noteworthy. A modern inscription records a semi-legendary episode, narrated by Livy, that happened near the former monument. The hero of this event was the centurion Virginius who killed his daughter whose honour was threatened by Appius Claudius, the decemvir. The **Basilica Fulvia-Aemilia** ⑤ , built in 179 B.C. by the censors Marcus Fulvius Nobilior and Marcus Aemilius Lepidus, taking from their families its name, replaced an earlier building on the site, perhaps also of public character. During the late Republican period, the Basilica was restored several times by members of the Aemilia family, so as to become a kind of commemorative monument

---

was in peril of his life. The Romans disbanded and fled towards the Palatine. Recovering from the blow, Romulus rushed before the fugitives to incite them to return to the assault, but since he could not stop them, he raised his hands to heaven invoking the name

of Jupiter to stop his army. Then many of Romulus' men felt their limbs bound for the shame of escaping before their king and, having stopped, set off to counter-attack the Sabines. 'The point where the Romans stopped to turn back is today the site

of the Temple of Jupiter Stator, that is translated as the "stayer". The arrival of the daughters of the Sabines who had been abducted by the Romans, but now dressed as the brides and mothers of their enemies, with their dishevelled and sorrowful supplications to both

armies, each related through them, put an end to the hostilities. The generals met to reach an accord and the place where this was drawn up 'today has the name of Comitius, from the verb *comire*, that in Latin means meet.'

for the gens. One of the most famous restorations was executed by another Marcus Aemilius Lepidus, consul in 78 B.C., who was responsible for the construction of a facade facing the Forum adorned with portraits of his ancestors on shields (*imagines clipeatae*) and the adoption, for the interior colonnade, of marble columns from Asia Minor (but commonly called African). Further restorations were carried out by other members of the same family with outside economic support: the work undertaken from 54 B.C. onwards was in fact financed by Caesar, whereas that of A.D. 22 received an indirect intervention from Tiberius. The last restoration of the Basilica dates back to the first half of the V century, after it

had been seriously damaged by a fire that has been linked to the sack of Rome by Alaric in A.D. 410. Although rebuilt several times, the Basilica Fulvia-Aemilia is the only building of its type which has been preserved from the Republican period down to the present day, since other Roman basilicas of that period (the Porcia, the Sempronia, the Opimia) were obliterated by later constructions. The three entrances to the Basilica (now closed to visitors) opened on the south side, towards the square, onto the Portico of Gaius and Lucius Caesar. Turning to the left, towards the short west side of the building are visible, under a modern shed, some remains of the primitive plan of the Basilica. They consist of the

foundation wall and the column bases of blocks of tuff from Grotta Oscura, some of which have quarry marks. The foundations reveal that, in its first building phase, the Basilica had three aisles, with colonnades that defined the lateral naves placed on the axes of the later ones, connected with the restoration of Marcus Aemilius Lepidus, while the central aisle still had not been given a greater width. The plan now visible in contrast has four aisles, with two smaller aisles on the north side and one on the south, while the central aisle, larger than the others, had a mezzanine floor with large windows opening onto it to illuminate the interior of the building. Among the decorative elements, besides the columns of Asiatic marble, of particular interest is the flooring of marble slabs belonging to the reconstruction undertaken to repair the damage caused by a fire in 14 B.C., and the late Republican reliefs with mythical scenes related to the origins of the city and the Aemilia family. These reliefs adorned the central aisle's architrave for a distance of 185 metres; the original fragments are kept in a section of the Antiquarium Forense not yet open to the

---

8. Basilica Fulvia-Aemilia, detail of the colonnade of the central aisle

9. Plaster cast of the frieze of the Basilica Fulvia-Aemilia: on the right, the murder of Tarpea is depicted

The cults of the Forum: Venus Cloacina

According to Livy, Cloacina was one of the titles of Venus. This name comes from the verb *cluere* (to purify). The myth of the foundation of her shrine is related to the Roman-Sabine war. Pliny

(*Natural History*, XV, 119-120) records that "... At the time of the foundation of Rome myrtles grew on the present site of the city, as tradition says that the Romans and the Sabines, before going to battle because of the rape of the Sabine maidens, laid down their

arms and purified themselves with springs of myrtle at the place now occupied by the statues of Venus Cloacina, *cluere* being the old word meaning "to cleanse". The myrthe has got purifying powers and was choosen because sacred to Venus, the goddess who presides

public. A plaster cast of a small part of the reliefs is now found on the north-east corner of the building and is visible coming down the modern entrance ramp. It

Mediaeval period stands out. Near the north-west corner of the Forum square, a small open area, almost a perfect square, opens onto the via Sacra; in this square are

Forum area covered in black stone, the **Niger Lapis** ⑥, an inauspicious place, near which Romulus was killed by the senators because of his despotic exploitation of power (and not the place where the King was buried, as the modern inscription placed at the end of the stairs under the enclosure states). We also know, from the ancient literary tradition, that Romulus was killed near a shrine dedicated to Vulcan, the *Volcanal*, so that it has been possible to connect the Archaic remains enclosed in the *Niger Lapis* with the site of this cult. These remains, dated to the first half of the VI century B.C., pertain to an open air sanctuary consisting of a tuff altar with three wings, near which was found a circular base, perhaps to support a statue, and a

depicts part of a complex scene that narrated the rape of the Sabine women and the culmination of the legend of Tarpea, when the young girl, having promised the Sabines to open the city gates in exchange for their ornaments on their left arms, was instead buried under the shields which the soldiers carried on that very arm. Beyond a metal fence are visible some remains, brought to light by recent excavations, among which an arcaded private building of the

found monuments of great interest, one beside the other, dated between the Archaic (VI century B.C.) and late Antique periods (III-IV century A.D.). The most significant monument of this area is an enclosure, defined by marble slabs fixed vertically, which contains a black stone pavement in the interior. The systemisation of this enclosure dates to the Sullan period and has been connected with what the ancient sources refer to when they describe a site in the

trapezoid cippus with a very fragmentary inscription in Archaic Latin. From an examination of the few intelligible remains of this text, it has been possible to identify the contents of the inscription with those of a sacred law that regulated the rituals carried out next to the altar under the control of the King, who is named in the third line of the inscription. We can infer the importance of the area where the *Volcanal* stood during the Regal and Republican periods

---

over unions." The myrtle of Cloacina was therefore a plant particularly preferred for use in weddings and thus its connection with the marital rape of the Sabine women is explained. The sanctuary of Cloacina was also positioned in front of the Basilica

Fulvia-Aemilia, precisely at the point in which the Cloaca Maxima entered the Forum, thus corresponding to the course of the Velabrum that, like all the other rivers, functioned as a boundary and, in this specific case, between the two warring peoples

who reached a truce beside it. A representation of this small border shrine is preserved on the coins of the Mussidia family, on which we can see a round platform adorned with a balustrade with two cult statues of the goddess, identified by the inscription *Cloacina*.

One of the two images seems to hold in one hand a myrtle branch, as a symbol of purification and the nuptial rites of passage, whereas the second represents the goddess as armed and thus as the guardian of the enclosure.

from the fact that the most important political buildings of the city were erected in its proximity. This complex consisted of the **Comitium** ⑦, the Curia Hostilia (the seats respectively of the popular assemblies and of the Senate meetings) and the tribune of the Rostra, from which the magistrates spoke in the performance of their duties. These buildings remained in use until the mid I century B.C., when the work undertaken by Caesar in this area of the Forum that was next to his new Forum, resulted in the disappearance of the Comitium and the construction of the Rostra ⑭ and the Curia Julia ⑧ in the places where they are now visible. The meeting place of the Senate built by Caesar, the **Curia Julia** ⑧, corresponds to the large brick building, in part restored in the modern period, that occupies the entire north side of the small square. The building work, begun by Caesar, was only completed by Augustus in 29 B.C. With respect to the position of the old Curia Hostilia, its remains were probably located under the adjacent Church of SS. Luca e Martina, whereas the new Curia occupied a site chosen to permit direct access to the Forum of Caesar, inaugurated in 46 B.C., where, while the

new Senate house was not yet ready, the senators often held their meetings. It seems that Caesar's habit of presiding at the Senate meetings from the steps of the Temple of Venus Genetrix which dominated

his Forum, was one of the reasons of his murder, that took place in another Curia used in those years, the one in the complex of Pompey in the Campus Martius.
The current state of the

Political sites in the Republican Forum

The principal site for meetings of political assemblies in Rome during the Republican period was the Comitium which occupied the area now delimited by the Arch of Septimius Severus, the

Forum of Caesar and the Basilica Fulvia-Aemilia. The precise topographical position has been reconstructed from the very scarce surviving remains, but above all from a passage of Pliny in which the operation of the Comitium is described as a kind of gigantic sun-dial

(*Natural History*, VII, 60). The description, thanks to the precision with which the position of buildings within the complex is indicated, has made it possible to reposition them ideally within the space. Strictly oriented according to cardinal points, beeing the space

Curia Julia belongs to a restoration carried out by Diocletian to repair the damage caused by a devastating fire in the reign of Carinus (A.D. 283); today the Curia Julia stands as one of the best preserved late Antique buildings of Rome. The surprising integrity of the monument is due to the fact that in the VII century it was transformed into the Church of S. Adriano. The external brick walls, lightened by relieving arches and interrupted by large windows in the facade, were originally covered with marble slabs on the lower sections, of which only scarce remains are still visible to the left of the entrance. Going up a short ramp of stairs, restored in recent times, we enter the hall of the Curia, whose bronze entrance door is a replica of the original one, transferred to the Basilica of S. Giovanni in Laterano in the XVII century. The large interior with its ceiling at a height of 21 metres, still preserves in large part the original pavement of the Diocletian period, made of marble slabs with inlays of precious polychrome marbles, such as porphyry and serpentine. This particularly luxurious type of pavement, called *opus sectile* from the technique employed, was used diffusely in Roman

buildings from the late Republican period on as an alternative to mosaic; in the late Antique period this kind of paving came to be used almost exclusively for public and religious buildings. On the left and right sides of the hall, three low steps served as supports for the chairs of the senators, who numbered about 300, whereas on the back wall, framed by two doors, was the president's platform with a base to support the statue of the goddess of Victory. The statue was removed from the Curia in A.D. 384-385 at the instance of St. Ambrosios, who, on that occasion, engaged in a close rhetorical debate with Quintus Aurelius Simmachus. A porphyry statue of a man in a toga, that now stands on the president's platform, was found immediately behind the Curia and is thought to belong to a monument erected in honour of the emperor Trajan. Three niches with alternating flat or arched

ceilings which are framed by small columns supported by corbels open along the walls of the two long sides; these niches were meant to hold honorific statues. Inside the hall are displayed two large marble reliefs, known as the **Plutei of Trajan**, which were found near a flower-bed where a fig tree, a vine and an olive have been replanted ㉖. The reliefs represent two important episodes in Trajan's activity in the Forum, of which a view of the entire south side is shown, permitting a reconstruction of the appearance of many buildings now only partially preserved. The relief on the left depicts a group of attendants who, in the presence of the emperor, are destroying the registers on which were transcribed debts contracted by Roman citizens to the Treasury; after the conquest of Dacia those debts were remitted. Behind the attendants are visible the buildings which formed the background of the scene: on

12. Reconstructed plan of the Comitium area in the Republican period

13. Interior of the Curia Julia

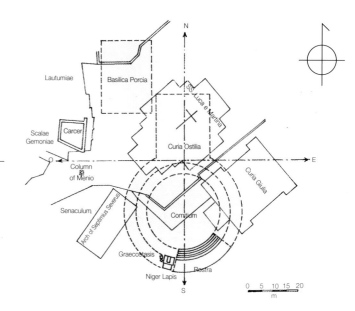

the left the remains of a tree (*ficus ruminalis*), a statue of Marsyas (dedicated from the profits of the fines paid by the usurers, probably by Lucius Marcius Censorinus, censor in 294 B.C., which quickly came to symbolise plebeian freedom from slavery as a result of debt), the arches of the Basilica Julia ③, an empty space corresponding to the *vicus Iugarius*, the Temple of Saturn ㉓ with its pronaos emphasised by six Ionic columns, a triumphal arch leading to the Capitol and finally another temple, of Vespasian and Titus ㉑, with the front adorned by six Corinthian columns. The relief on the right, in contrast, represents Trajan at the moment of the institution of the *alimenta*, economic aid designed to support Roman children of needy families. The emperor, surrounded by men in togas, is seated on a platform with an allegory of Italy with a child in her arms in front of him. Here too, from right to left, are recognisable the Marsyas, the *ficus ruminalis*, the arches of Basilica Julia, an empty space connected to the *vicus Tuscus* (whose name records the existence of an area near the Forum inhabited by Etruscans), the Temple of the Castores ㉟ with a Corinthian colonnade in front of it, an arch, perhaps the one dedicated by Augustus

consecrated by the augurs (the *templum*), the Comitium was comprised of a central square for meetings of the popular assemblies in the most ancient form of the comitia curiata; the Curia, where the members of the Senate assembled was on its north side whereas on its south side was the tribune from which the magistrates spoke. This platform took on the name of *Rostra* only after the rostra of the Latin ships captured at Antium in 338 B.C. were hung on its sides. On the south side of the square there was also the *Graecostasis*, the platform from which foreign ambassadors spoke, especially Greeks, thus the name. Stratigraphic excavations completed in the Comitium area permit an understanding of the main transformations which occurred in this important political site. The first paved level dates to the end of the VII century B.C. and was built at the same time as the first *Regia*, whereas the second pavement (around 570 B.C.) belongs to the sacred complex under the *Niger Lapis*, identified with the *Volcanal*. The orators' tribune was

built for the first time at the beginning of the Republican period and then, in its enlargement around the middle of the IV century B.C., received, as we have already said, the rostra of the Latin ships. In the first half of the III century B.C., in imitation of Greek *ekklesiasteria* (buildings also intended for meetings of political assemblies), the Comitium took the form of a round square with internal steps; this form was preserved until the end of the Republic. At the same time, Valerius Messalla, victor over the Carthaginians and the Syracusans in the first Punic war, brought from Catania the first sun clock (263 B.C.). The Comitium became a prototype which was reproduced in the Latin colonies founded by the Romans between the end of the IV century and the first half of the III century B.C. (*Fregellae, Alba Fucens, Cosa, Paestum*) and that spread throughout the Italic region: at Pietrabbondante, in the heart of Molise, when the Pentri Samnites built the headquarters of their provincial assembly in monumental form, placing it under the sacred sign,

in the Forum as a monument to his victory over Antonius at Actium in 31 B.C. ㉞ and finally a suggestus with rostra attached, identified as the tribune, situated in front of the Temple of Divus Julius ㉝, adorned with the rostra of Antonius' ships. The opposite sides of both reliefs are adorned with figures of a bull, a sheep and a pig, the animals designated for solemn sacrifices (*suovetaurilia*).

As already noted, there are **Honorific Bases** of statues as well as the remains of a round fountain basin in the small square. On the left, facing the Curia, is the base of a statue dedicated by Maxentius (whose name has been inscribed) to Mars ⑨, the mythical father of Romulus, who had been worshipped here since the most ancient times and whose name had been taken by the son of the emperor. Almost in correspondence with the *Niger Lapis*, but along the left side of the via Sacra, a large inscription, placed on a reused marble base, commemorates the victory of the emperors Arcadius, Honorius and Theodosius over the hordes led by Radagaisus in A.D. 405 ⑩; the fifth line from the bottom gives the inscribed name of the conquering general, Stilicon, executed in A.D. 408 by order of Honorius.

with their grandiose Theatre-Temple complex they replicated, surely consciously, the plan of the Curia-Comitium complex of the Roman world. Extensive modifications were made in the Comitium area during the Sullan period, when the construction of a larger Curia capable of accommodating the increased number of Senators was initiated and a black marble pavement sealed off the Archaic *Volcanal*. It was the work of Caesar to transform the Curia of Sulla into the Temple of *Felicitas* and to begin construction of the new Curia Julia, completed by Augustus, shifting the building to the east almost as an appendix to his new Forum. This resulted in the shifting of the Rostra further to the west and the elimination of the *Graecostasis*.

14. Plutei of Trajan, preserved inside the Curia Julia: scene depicting the destruction of the debt registers

15. Plutei of Trajan: scene depicting the institution of the alimenta

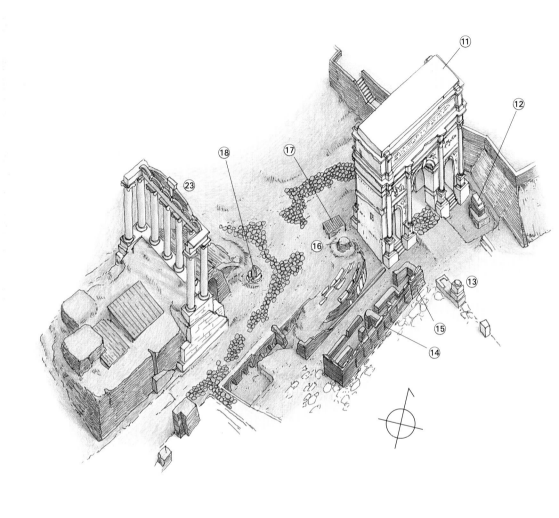

11 Arch of Septimius Severus
12 Base of Constantius II
13 Decennalia Base
14 Imperial Rostra
15 *Rostra Vandalica*
16 *Mundus/Umbilicus Urbis*
17 Altar of Saturn
18 *Miliarium Aureum*
23 Temple of Saturn with the Aerarium

THE WEST SIDE OF THE FORUM: FROM THE ARCH OF SEPTIMIUS SEVERUS TO THE TEMPLE OF SATURN

The north corner of this side of the square is dominated by the huge mass of the **Arch of Septimius Severus** ⑪. In front of it, on the right, stands the **base of the equestrian statue** ⑫ dedicated to the emperor Constantius II to commemorate his defeat of the usurper Magnentius in A.D. 352. The Arch of Septimius Severus, celebrating the Imperial victories over the Parthians, was constructed in A.D. 203 at the point where the via Sacra begins its ascent towards the Capitoline hill where the closing ceremonies of the triumph took place. This monument, completely faced with marble, has three openings (each one of which is framed by Corinthian columns on podiums) and is surmounted by a tall attic where the dedicatory inscription is still legible. In the fourth line from the top, the name and titles of the

second son of Septimius Severus, Geta, were obliterated after his murder, commissioned by his brother Caracalla, and replaced with the words: *optimis fortissimisque principibus* (to the best and strongest emperors). The decoration of the main sides of the arch, which face respectively the Forum and the Capitol, is very rich and elaborate (to enjoy the best view of the side facing the Capitol, it is advisable to stand on the terrace in front of the Church of SS. Luca e Martina). The podium of each column was adorned with figures of Roman soldiers guarding Parthian prisoners, whereas on the sides of the central archivault there are two winged Victories bearing trophies that point towards the central keystone, on which Mars is depicted. On the sides of the smaller passageways, which are only accessible on foot, two statues

probably representing river deities are sculptured, while above them runs a very small frieze, now barely recognisable, that represented the triumphal procession that accompanied the emperor onto the Capitol. The space between the side passages and the cornice supported by the

16. Arch of Septimius Severus, east side

17. Arch of Septimius Severus, west side: detail of the attic with the dedicatory inscription

The panels of the Arch of Septimius Severus

The visual narrative of Septimius Severus' deeds during the two Parthian campaigns begins on the left panel on the Forum side, continues on the right panel of the same

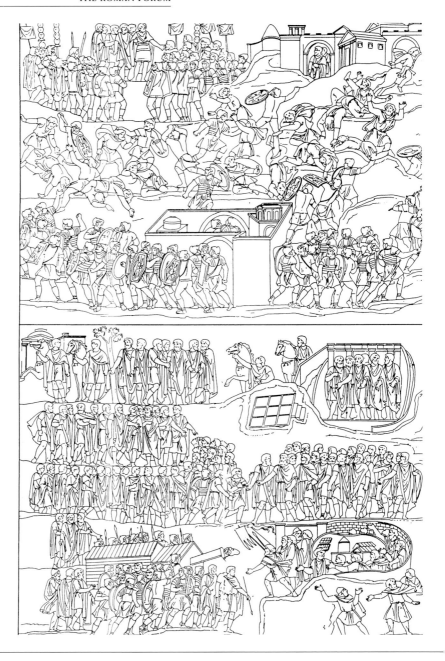

18. Graphic reconstruction of the panels of the Arch of Septimius Severus on the side facing the Forum: on the top, the left panel; on the bottom, the right panel

19. Graphic reconstruction of the panels of the Arch of Septimius Severus on the side facing the Capitol: on the top, the left panel; on the bottom, the right panel

side then proceeds on the two panels of the side facing the Capitol, following throughout the same order from left to right. The relief of each panel must be read from the bottom to the top. The left panel on the Forum side contains a schematic but effective

synthesis of the events of the first Parthian war (A.D. 195) set out in three registers: below, the departure of the Roman army from their camp; in the centre, a battle scene; above, the flight of the Parthian king Vologese (on the right) and Septimius Severus addressing his

troops (on the left). The story of the second victorious campaign (A.D. 197-198) begins in the right panel on the Forum side: in the lower register, the Roman attack with war machines (a battering ram) on the city of Edessa, that throws open its gates and sends forward dignitaries and standards in order to surrender; in the middle one, the submission of the king of the Osroeni, Abgar (on the right) and Septimius Severus address to the army; in the top register, a war council within a fortified camp (on the right) and the departure to enter the hostile territory (on the left). Moving on to the panels on the side towards the Capitol, the left panel represents the attack on Seleucia on the Tigris with the Parthians escaping on horseback (below) and their submission before the Emperor (above), while the right panel depicts on the lower register the attack and fall of the city of Ctesifonte, from which the king Vologese is escaping (on the far right of the register) and on the top register, Septimius Severus' final oration in front of the conquered city.

columns includes large relief panels that showed, like the paintings exhibited during the triumph, the main episodes of the military exploits undertaken in Parthian territory.

On the left side of the via Sacra, re-erected on a modern brick foundation, is found an honorific column base, known as the **Decennalia Base** ⑬, that commemorates the tenth anniversary of the power of the Caesars in the Tetrarchy (A.D. 303); with this new Imperial institution, Diocletian attempted to solve the problem of succession, having put side by side the two supreme emperors (the Augusti), who ruled the Eastern and Western parts of the Empire, supported by two younger rulers (the Caesars), who will ascend to the highest authority when the Augusti voluntarily retire to private life. This base formed part of a more complex monument composed of four additional columns, one to each Augustus and each Caesar with a statue dedicated to Jupiter in the centre. The side of the base, facing the via Sacra, represent two winged Victories carrying a shield, on which the commemorative inscriptions of the tenth anniversary of the reign of

the Caesars appears: *Caesarum decennalia feliciter.* The east side, in the direction of the Forum square, is devoted to a procession of senators, while on the opposite side, appear the sacrificial bull, sheep and pig, accompanied by attendants and a man in a toga. The main side was on the south where the key moment of the entire ceremony was depicted: the Caesar as protagonist of the scene, in the middle of the composition, appears in front of an altar in the act of making a libation, while a Victory flies to crown him. In front of this figure are found, besides an attendant, a priest with pointed headgear (*flamen Martialis*), a nude figure with a helmet (Mars) and a bearded figure in a toga, with which the Augustus is identified; on the opposite side, behind the Caesar, in addition to a man in a toga identified as a personification of the Senate, the seated goddess Roma and the radiate head of the Sun god appear.

Entering into the paved space of the square, one sees on the right a large podium that occupies almost the entire short west side; partially reconstructed in the modern period, part of the original masonry made of square tuff blocks has been preserved on the lower section. This monument is identified with the Augustan restyling of the large great orators' tribune, the **Imperial Rostra** ⑭, erected in this position by Caesar around the middle of the I century B.C.; it replaced the tribune used throughout the entire Republican period that was demolished during the intensive work undertaken by Caesar in the area of the Comitium. The only remnant of the Rostra of the Caesarean period is the hemicycle visible behind the podium, that with its curvilinear shape recalled the form of the Republican Rostra included in the Comitium; the rectilinear structure belonging to the Augustan reconstruction still preserves the depressions into which were placed the rostra

20. Decennalia base, east side: procession of senators

21. Decennalia base, west side: the bull, the sheep, and the pig destined for sacrifice

from Antium, that were transferred from the older tribune originally in the Comitium. To the extreme north of the base (to the right, facing the Capitol) stands a stretch of masonry in opus latericium of rather rough workmanship, on which is found part of an inscription celebrating the naval victory over the Vandals of the praefect of the city Junius Valentinus around A.D. 470; it is therefore probable that the restoration of the Rostra in brick masonry should be ascribed to him, but the name given to this part of the restoration, the **Rostra Vandalica** ⑮, is modern.

In the area of the square near the Rostra just described, two series of small wells with different orientations are visible: the first series, east-west oriented, with three rectangular openings with a border of modern bricks (one is covered with a grille) correspond to some of the votive wells that marked the boundaries of the area of the Comitium, consecrated by the Augurs; the second series, north-south oriented and just in front of facade of the

Augustan Rostra ⑭, pertains precisely to the Forum square, whose space was also ritually defined, probably when electoral activities were transferred here from the Comitium in the mid II century B.C.

Behind the hemicycle of the Caesarean rostra, a rounded core of opus latericium stands against the south pier of the Arch of Septimius Severus. It belongs to a very important monument in the Forum, strictly connected by the ancient tradition to all the rituals of Rome's foundation, the so-called **Mundus** ⑯, referred to by some sources as the *Umbilicus Urbis*. This place was considered the centre of the city and the point where the living world was in contact, through a deep cleft in the ground, with the underworld, inhabited by infernal beings and the shades of the dead. From the Republican period, it seems that the monument was divided into two different parts: the lower section was

the *Mundus* proper and to it were connected special expiatory rites to the underworld gods, while the upper part constituted the *Umbilicus Urbis*. To this part of the monument belongs the fragment of architectural decoration still visible, which rests on the brick core and pertains to a restoration of the Severian period executed with decorative elements characteristic of the final phase of the II century B.C. In the same site, in the area between the Arch of Septimius Severus ⑪ and the Temple of Saturn ㉓, are found other buildings of small size, but of great religious or symbolic significance. Under a modern roof, again placed next to the south pier of the Arch of Septimius Severus ⑪, there is a cult area in part cut into the living rock and in part constructed of blocks of the soft Roman tuff called cappellaccio. This cult area has been identified with the **Altar of Saturn** ⑰, whose construction, perhaps in the

22. Imperial Rostra. Augustan restoration of the orators' tribune; in the foreground the so-called Rostra Vandalica are visible

23. Umbilicus Urbis

24. Capital with rams belonging to the interior decoration of the Temple of Concord

VI century B.C., predates that of the temple dedicated to the same god. Almost in front of what remains of the steps of the Temple of Saturn, it is possible to see the fragments of a column base with palmette decorations placed practically on axis with the *Mundus*; these sparse remains belong to the **Miliarium Aureum** ⑱, a monument built by Augustus in 20 B.C., on which the distances between Rome and the main cities of the Empire were recorded and which originally consisted of a column faced in gilded bronze. In front of this monument are visible several arches in opus quasi reticulatum, heavily restored in modern times, identified on a sign as the Arch of Tiberius, but actually only the substructures of the slope going up to the Capitol.

The area to the west of the Arch of Septimius Severus ⑪, that has as its architectural backdrop the arches of the *Tabularium* ⑲, is not open to the public and therefore the view from the terraces along the modern roads leading to the Capitol is recommended, beginning from the building to the left of the *Tabularium* looking towards the Forum.

The myths of the Forum: the *Mundus*

Plutarch, *Romulus*, XI, 1-2.
" Romulus buried Remus, together with his foster-fathers, in the *Remoria*, and then set himself to building his city, after summoning from Tuscany men who prescribed all the details in accordance with certain sacred ordinances and writings, and taught them to him as in a religious rite. A circular trench was dug around what is now the Comitium, and in this were deposited first-fruits of all things the use of which was sanctioned by custom as good and by nature as necessary; and finally, every man brought a small portion of the soil of his native land, and these were cast in among the first fruits and mingled with them. They call this trench, as they do the heavens, by the name of "*mundus*". Then taking this as a centre, they marked out the city in a circle round it."

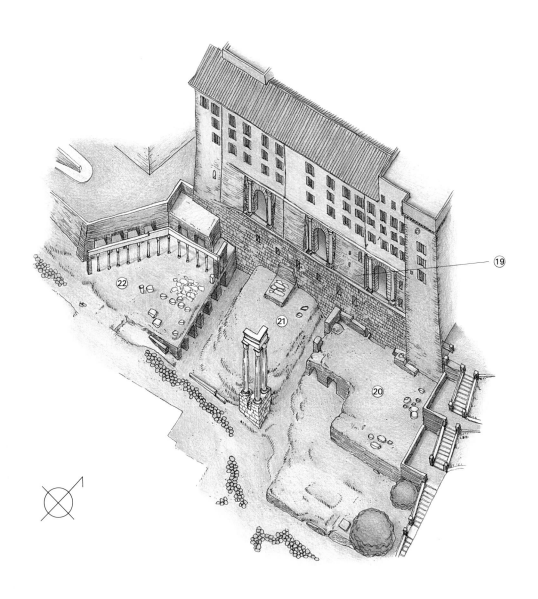

The core in opus caementicium now visible is all that remains of the podium where the massive building of the **Temple of Concord** ⑳ once stood. According to tradition, the Temple was erected by Camillus from 367 B.C. onwards in memory of the reconciliation between patricians and plebeians that occurred on the day after the promulgation of the Liciniae-Sestiae laws that established political equality between the two components of Roman society (but some modern critics are sceptical of the historical truth of this tradition, identifying the praetor of 218 B.C., Lucius Manlius, as the builder of the Temple). In 121 B.C., after the end of the political disorder that culminated in the death of the tribune of the people, Gaius Gracchus, the consul Lucius Opimius rebuilt the temple and put a basilica beside it, called Opimia after him. The current form of the Temple is due to the restoration undertaken by Tiberius between 7 B.C. and A.D. 10; to better exploit the narrow space between the Altar of Saturn ⑰ and the *Tabularium*, the Temple assumed a quite extraordinary shape, with the cella set transversely to the main axis and a pronaos consisting of

an avant-corps with six columns along the front. Inside the cella, adorned with columns surmounted by elaborate Corinthian capitals with figures of pairs of rams (one example is preserved in a section of the Antiquarium Forense closed to visitors), Tiberius installed an extremely rich collection of Greek sculpture, collected during the years of his voluntary exile in Rhodes, thus transforming the temple into a kind of museum. The last restoration of this building, verified by an inscription now lost, was undertaken in the late Antique period. Near the Temple of Concord, three marble Corinthian columns indicate the presence of another sacred building. An inscription, that is now very fragmentary, but whose contents were transcribed in full in the Mediaeval period, permits the identification of the building with the **Temple of Vespasian and Titus** ㉑; completed under Domitian in the form of a temple with a pronaos with six columns along the front and two columns on the long sides, the building was restored during the reign of Septimius Severus and Caracalla. Above the surviving part of the lateral colonnade, a section of the architrave is still preserved, adorned with

sacrificial instruments (patera, knife, axe, amphora, spiked helmet, aspergillum, bucranium). At the south end of the *Tabularium* (to the right, looking in the direction of the Forum) is annexed a small portico, shaped like an obtuse angle, emphasised by Corinthian columns. Here too, the inscription on the architrave allows a clarification of the function of this monument, in which the statues of the *Dei Consentes* were preserved (the counsellor gods, twelve in number, who were probably the supreme gods in the Roman pantheon and whose cult site near the Forum is recorded from the Republican period). The modern name given to the building in his complex, the **Portico of Dei Consentes** ㉒, comes from them. The columns of the portico, in cipollino marble (from the Greek quarries of Euboea), have Corinthian capitals decorated on the sides with reliefs representing trophies; their production dates to the end of the I century A.D., even if the above mentioned inscription records that the entire building was restored in A.D. 367 by the city praefect Vectius Agorius Pretestatus, one of the last official opponents of Christianity. To the same late Antique restoration belong six rooms in opus latericium situated behind the columns, where, perhaps in pairs, the statues of the gods were displayed.

Returning to the buildings placed in the more immediate vicinity to the short west side of the Forum, the entire south corner is still dominated by the remains of the **Temple of Saturn** ㉓. On a high podium, covered in marble blocks on the lower part and travertine above, the columns of the pronaos stand, six of grey granite on the front and two of red granite on the short sides, with Ionic capitals on top. The architrave, adorned on its interior face with a palmette decoration, bears a dedicatory inscription that records the temple's restoration after a fire, almost certainly the one that devastated much of the Forum in A.D. 283. However, the building's first construction dates back to a much earlier period, the first years of the V century B.C., only a little later than the construction of the impressive Temple of Jupiter Optimus Maximus. A symbol of the new born Republic, that wished to refer to itself as the Golden Age, when this god reigned on the Capitol, The Temple of Saturn housed the Aerarium, the State Treasury, whose headquarters

has been recognised in the cavity made in the interior of the massive podium in opus caementicium. Nothing remains of this first building, whereas the entire massive podium and its revetment have been connected with the restoration begun by Lucius Munatius Plancus in 42 B.C.

25. Portico of the Dei Consentes

26. The columns of the Temple of Saturn's pronaos, seen from the interior

*27. Temple of Saturn;
below, the decorated
architrave of the Temple
of Vespasian and Titus*

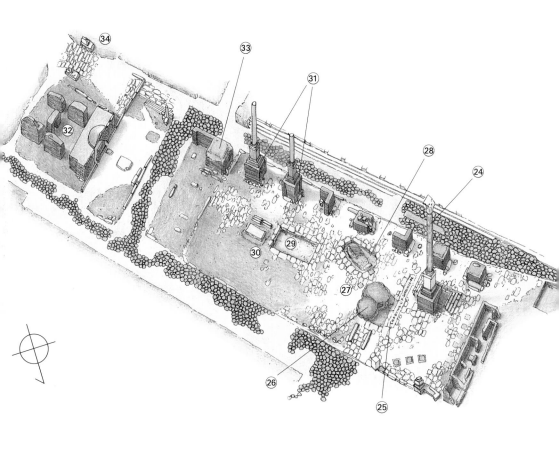

24 Column of Phocas
25 Inscription of *L. Naevius Surdinus*
26 *Ficus, olea, vitis* (fig tree, olive, vine)
27 Small well-heads
28 *Lacus Curtius*
29 *Doliola*
30 Late Antique *Doliola*
31 Honorific columns
32 Temple of Divus Julius
33 *Rostra ad Divi Iulii*
34 Actium Arch

THE CENTRAL SQUARE:
FROM THE COLUMN OF PHOCAS
TO THE TEMPLE OF DIVUS JULIUS

In front of the Imperial Rostra ⑭, on a high square brick podium against which the remains of a marble stairway lean, stands the *Column of Phocas* ㉔. The commemorative monument, that according to the inscription on its plinth consisted of a column surmounted by a gold statue, was dedicated on the 1st of August in 608 A.D., by the exarch of Italy, Smaradgo, to the emperor Phocas, who ascended to the throne in 602 A.D., after having killed his predecessor Mauritius and his five sons. Actually, the high honorific column in the Corinthian order (13,60 metres) probably belonged to a commemorative monument of the II century A.D. Apart from testifying in an almost complete manner to the appearance of the honorific columns that filled the Forum space from the mid-Republican period onwards (the earliest mentioned in the sources is the one erected in honour of Gaius Menius, the consul who was victorious over the Latins at Antium in 338 B.C.), the importance of the Column of Phocas resides in the fact that it represents the latest monument,

chronologically, erected in the Forum. After A.D. 608 the progressive and irreversible abandonment of the monumental centre of the city began, and as a result only Christian buildings, built at the expense of the pagan monuments, were constructed.

Immediately to the east of the Column of Phocas, is the **Large Inscription** ㉕, in bronze letters, that commemorated this paving of the square, carried out by

---

28. General view of the central square of the Forum from the north-east; in the foreground the columns of the late Antique restoration of the Portico of Gaius and Lucius Caesar

29. Column of Phocas

The gladiators in the Forum

With the sole exception of the first gladiatorial game (*munus*) organised in 264 B.C. in the Forum Boarium by Decimus Junius Brutus in honour of his dead father, throughout the entire

Republican period, the *munera* were held in the Roman Forum, where temporary stands were erected around the square. Although temporary, they were solid enough to accommodate a large number of spectators and, if necessary, to support the

awnings that protected the audience from the excessive heat of the sun. These awnings are explicitly mentioned with respect to the games given by Julius Caesar in 46 B.C. (Pliny, *Natural History*, XIX, 23). In the Caesarean period, at a depth of one meter under

periods and the pavement in tuff slabs dated to the Republican period.

A tuff foundation of dodecagonal shape covered by a modern roof was intentionally respected by the pavement and therefore was part of an earlier systemisation of this area. The foundation, belonging to a well, together with the entire space surrounding it, constitutes the complex known as the **Lacus Curtius** ㉘, an area which remained marshy down to the Augustan period. The name of the complex was connected with the story of a hero named *Curtius* represented on a marble relief of the mid I century B.C., that has a second inscription of *Surdinus* on the back side (a cast of which now rests on the edge of the basin). Almost in the centre of the square, there is a large cavity with walls of opus caementicium, inside which are found three travertine blocks with a square hole in the centre of each. During the excavations that in 1904 brought this section to light, in the hollow of a fourth block, found at a lower level than the other three, a deposit of vases dated to the VII century B.C. was found perfectly preserved and therefore intentionally placed there. This discovery has

the urban praetor L. Naevius Surdinus during the principate of Augustus, which was in large part reintegrated into the travertine pavement in 1955. In an area, left unpaved even in antiquity, **a fig tree**, **a vine and an olive** ㉖ have been replanted that Pliny the Elder, as explained in the modern inscription, recorded near the central space of the Forum. Between this unpaved section of the square and the *Lacus Curtius* ㉘ are found several square **small well-heads** ㉗, now fenced and covered by gratings, that were executed at the same time as an earlier pavement which dates to the time of Caesar. The function of these wells, that were covered over by the later paving executed

by *Surdinus* during the Augustan period, has been clarified thanks to the relation they have with an intricate system of subterranean passages under the square: like the subterranean tunnels under the amphitheatres, these passages and wells constituted the service rooms utilised for the gladiatorial games, that until the Augustan period utilised the central space of the Forum as an arena.

To the south-east of these wells, a trapezoidal area is visible, that still preserves the remains of three different pavings of the Forum square; from top to bottom, are recognisable the two travertine pavements implemented respectively in the Augustan and Caesarean

30. The fig tree, the olive and the vine now replanted in the central square of the Forum

the travertine pavement of the Forum square, an orthogonal system of tunnels was built (2.40 metres high, 1.50 metres wide, with tuff walls and vaults in opus incertum); the longitudinal axis measured 75 metres and ended in square manoeuvre rooms, with

vaulted ceilings, in which excavators of the last century found remains of wooden hoists, probably used to lift to the Forum level heavy objects necessary for the games. This reticulate system of subterranean galleries, accessible from the pavement level through

wells with square openings, went out of use in the Augustan period, when the new pavement of the Forum, implemented by *Surdinus* closed those openings. This observation represents a clear archaeological confirmation of what was

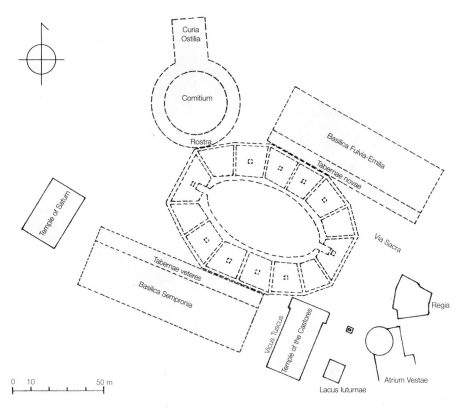

already known from the literary tradition, according to which the organisation of gladiatorial games in the Forum square ended in 7 B.C., the year in which the *munus* offered by Augustus in memory of his son-in-law Agrippa was held in the splendid

and prestigious setting of the *Saepta Iulia* in the Campus Martius. From then on, this building was preferred to the Forum square for all the performances that could not be carried out in the Amphitheatre of Statilius Taurus, which was only constructed in 29 B.C.

31. Relief depicting the legend of Mettius Curtius

32. Reconstructed plan of the temporary tribunes erected in the Forum in the pre-Augustan period

The myths of the Forum: the *Lacus Curtius*

To explain the name of the *Lacus Curtius*, a hollow or bog in the centre of the Roman Forum, that was drained in the Augustan period and turned into a kind of

column, a brick building, largely dismantled in 1874, marks the site of the **Rostra ad Divi Iulii** ㉝, the orators' tribune situated in front of the Temple of the deified Caesar, from which were proclaimed the funeral orations of many members of the Julio-Claudian family. The building technique used for the core of this tribune shows that it was totally rebuilt in the late Antique period. On the short east side of the Forum square, beyond the byway that joined the via Sacra with the road that went along the south side of the Forum square, the scarce remains of the **Temple of Divus Julius** ㉜ are preserved; it was dedicated by Augustus on the 18th of August in 29 B.C., to the deified Caesar, his adoptive father. The search for precious building materials that was carried out in this site during the Renaissance, spared only the core of the podium, constructed of opus caementicium with the integration of tuff fragments. The most characteristic element of this building is the hemicycle in the front part of the podium. The hemicycle, later closed off by a wall of tuff blocks, includes the cement core of a round altar placed perhaps on the spot where the body of Caesar was cremated. The

been connected to the area of the *Doliola* ㉙, the place where, according to one tradition, the Vestal Virgins buried the ritual vases at the time of the Gallic invasion, but that the scholar Varro considered a cult area of most ancient origins, established by the king Numa Pompilius, where sacred objects belonging to him had been buried. The area underwent several restorations, the latest of which, probably of the Constantinian period, is verified by a base placed against the east side of the cavity ㉚. From the same excavations undertaken in

this area come the two burials without funerary equipment now displayed in room III of the Antiquarium Forense. The entire south side of the square was occupied by six high brick bases to support **Honorific Columns** ㉛ erected in the late Antique period. Two of them, situated on the far east side, were re-erected at the end of the XIX century, using shafts of grey granite and white marble found in the vicinity; the loss of the dedicatory inscriptions prevents us from verifying to whom these honorific monuments were dedicated. Immediately after the granite

well-head rising on the dry ground, and into which offerings in the honour of the Emperor were thrown, Roman tradition appealed to aetiological myths that focused on a hero named *Curtius*. According to one version, the Sabine knight *Mettius Curtius* saved

himself with difficulty from the mire into which he had fallen when fighting Romulus; whereas, according to another legend it was the heroic Roman knight *M. Curtius* who, in 362 B.C., obeying an oracle, jumped with his armour into an abyss that had suddenly

opened in the Forum in order to save his country. But the most probable narrative is the one told by Livy, according to which the consul of 445 B.C., *C. Curtius*, by order of the senate, consecrated and fenced an area struck by lightning. In 1553, a

Greek marble relief representing the legend was found near the monument, to which it certainly belonged; this relief which dates to the Sullan or Caesarean period is now preserved in the Palazzo dei Conservatori.

only surviving elements of the architectural decoration of the Temple, that, as is known from the images on coins, had six Corinthian columns along the front and two corresponding on the long sides, are some fragments of coffered ceiling placed along the north side of the podium which are decorated with palmettes, crowns, and bunches of grapes and a few remains of the frieze with winged Victories emerging from acanthus spirals; they are preserved in part of the Antiquarium Forense still closed to visitors. To the south of the Temple of Divus Julius (to the right of its facade) are visible traces of the pilasters that supported the vaults of a triumphal arch, identified with the **Actium Arch** ㉞. This monument was inaugurated from Augustus in 29 B.C., (the same year as the Temple of Divus Julius nearby) to commemorate his victory over Antonius and Cleopatra in 31 B.C. and took the place of an earlier triumphal arch that he had built to commemorate the positive result of the battle of Naulochus, engaged against the powerful fleet of Sestus Pompey in 36 B.C. In the new atmosphere of political peace, the substitution of the Arch of Naulochus with

the one of Actium reveals Augustus' intention to remove from the city's political centre all record of the civil wars in which he was a protagonist in the period of the triumvirate with Antonius and Lepidus. Instead, he left the task of celebrating his exploits to monuments commemorating his victorious war against the Queen of Egypt and Antonius, a well-orchestrated propaganda campaign that presented it as a war between Romans and Eastern barbarians. A similar phenomenon is documented in these same years by the monuments erected on the

Palatine, where the Temple of Apollo, built to commemorate the victory at Naulochus as well, received the rostra captured from the Egyptian ships of Antonius. The appearance of the arch is largely known from coins of the Imperial period, where it is depicted as a triple arch, with an arched central opening while the side passages had flat ceilings and triangular tympanums. Probably the inscribed panels containing the consular and triumphal fasti, now displayed in the Museo dei Conservatori, were on the interior of this arch.

33. Area of the Doliola: the travertine reliquary containing a deposit of vases from the VII century B.C. at the time of discovery

34. Honorific Columns on the south side of the central square of the Forum

35. Podium of the Temple
of Divus Julius; on the
right, the Temple of Vesta

36. The Temple of Divus
Julius seen from the south-
east; the remains of the
Actium Arch of Augustus
are visible beside it

The Funeral of Caesar

(Suetonius, *Life of Divine Caesar*, 84-85)
"When the funerals where announced, a pyre was erected in the Campus Martius near the tomb of Julia, and on the Rostra a gilded shrine was placed, made after the model of the temple of Venus Gentrix; within was a bier of ivory with coverlets of purple and gold, and at its head a pillar hung with the robe in which he was slain.(...). At the funeral games, to rouse pity and indignation at his death, these words from the "Contest for the Arms" of Pacuvius were sung: "Saved I these men that they might murder me?" and words of a like purport from the "Electra" of Atilius. Instead of a eulogy the consul Antonius caused a herald to recite the decree of the Senate in which it had voted Caesar all divine and human honours at once, and likewise the oath with which they had all pledged themselves to watch over his personal safety; to which he added a very few words of his own. The bier was carried to the Rostra in the Forum by magistrates and ex-magistrates; and while some were urging to be burned in the temple of Jupiter of the Capitol, and others in the Hall of Pompey, on a sudden two beings with swords by their sides and brandishing a pair of darts set fire to it with blazing torches, and at once the throng of bystanders heaped upon it dry branches, the judgment seats with the benches, and whatever else could serve as an offering. Then the musicians and the actors tore off their robes, which they had taken from the equipment of the triumphs and put on for the occasion, rent them to bits and threw them into the flames, and the veterans of the legions the arms with which they had adorned themselves for the funeral; many of the women too, offered up the jewels which they wore and the amulets and robes of their children.(....). Afterwards the people set up in the Forum a solid column of Numidian marble almost twenty feet high, and inscribed upon it, "To the Father of his Country". At the foot of this they continued for a long time to sacrifice, make vows, and settle some of their disputes by an oath in the name of Caesar."

Funeral eulogy of Caesar

(W. Shakespeare, *Julius Caesar*, Act III, scene II)
Antony: "Friends, Romans, countrymen, lend me your ears;/ I come to bury Caesar, not to praise him./ The evil that men do lives after them, / The good is oft interred with their bones;/ So let it be with Caesar: The noble Brutus/ Hath told you Caesar was ambitious./ If it were so, it was a grievous fault,/ And grievously hath Caesar answered it. / Here, under leave of Brutus and the rest -/ For Brutus is an honourable man;/ So are they all, all honourable men-/ Come I to speak in Caesar's funeral./ He was my friend, faithful and just to me;/ But Brutus says he was ambitious, / And Brutus is an honourable man./ He hath brought many captives home to Rome,/ Whose ransoms did the general coffers fill:/ Did this in Caesar seem ambitious?/ ... You all did see that on the Lupercal/ I thrice presented him a kingly crown,/ Which he did thrice refuse. Was this ambition?/ Yet Brutus says he was ambitious,/ And sure he is an honourable man./ I speak not to disprove what Brutus spoke/ But here I am to speak what I do know./ You all did love him once, not without cause; / What cause witholds you then to mourn for him?/...But yesterday the word of Caesar might/ Have stood against the world; now lies he there,/ And none so poor to do him reverence./ O masters! If I were disposed to stir/ Your hearts and minds to mutiny and rage,/ I should do Brutus wrong, and Cassius wrong,/ Who, you all know, are honourable men./ I will not do them wrong; I rather choose/ To wrong the dead, to wrong myself and you,/ Than I will wrong such honourable men./ But here's a parchment with the seal of Caesar;/ I found it in his closet; 'tis his will./ Let but the commons hear this testament,/ Which, pardon me, I do not mean to read, / And they would go and kiss dead Caesar's wounds,/ and dip their napkins in his sacred blood,/...If you have tears, prepare to shed them now./ You all do know this mantle. I remember/ The first time ever Caesar put it on;/ 'Twas on a summer's evening in his tent,/ that day he overcame the Nervii./ Look, in this place ran Cassius' dagger through;/ See what a rent the envious Casca made;/ Through this, the well-beloved Brutus stabbed;/ And as he plucked his cursed steel away,/ Mark how the blood of Caesar followed it,/ As rushing out of doors, to be resolved/ If Brutus so unkindly knocked or no;/ For Brutus, as you know was Caesar's angel./....Kind souls, what weep you when you but behold/ Our Caesar's vesture wounded? Look you here,/ Here is himself, marred, as you see, with traitors./....For I have neither wit, nor words, nor worth,/ Action, nor utterance, nor the power of speech/ To stir men's blood; I only speak right on./ I tell you that which you yourselves do know,/ Show you sweet Cesar's wounds, poor poor dumb mouths,/And bid them speak for me. But were I Brutus,/ And Brutus Antony, there were an Antony/ Would ruffle up your spirits, and put a tongue/ In every wound of Caesar that should move/ The stones of Rome to rise and mutiny."

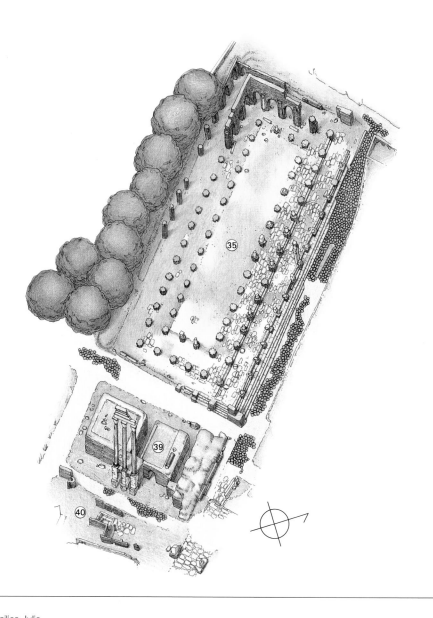

㉟ Basilica Julia

㊴ Temple of the Castores

㊵ *Lacus Iuturnae*

THE SOUTH SIDE OF THE FORUM:
FROM THE BASILICA JULIA
TO THE LACUS IUTURNAE

The construction of the **Basilica Julia** ㉟ was initiated by Caesar around 54 B.C., but work continued in the principate of Augustus. Destroyed by a fire shortly after its inauguration, the basilica was completely rebuilt and dedicated to the adoptive sons of the emperor, Gaius and Lucius Caesar, in A.D. 12. Like many other buildings in the Forum, it suffered profound damage in the fire of A.D. 283; the restoration, undertaken a few years later, during the Diocletianic period, does not seem to have altered the original appearance of the basilica, that preserved its characteristic arcaded facade, the appearance of which is known from the relief decoration of the Plutei of Trajan, now displayed in the Curia Julia ⑧.

This area of the Forum had been already chosen as the site of a building of the same type; in 169 B.C., Tiberius Sempronius Gracchus, the father of the two famous

37. Basilica Julia seen from the Capitol

tribunes of the people, built on this same site the Basilica Sempronia that, with its complex of shops on the side facing the Forum (the *tabernae veteres*), was placed as a symmetrical construction to the Basilica Fulvia-Aemilia ⑤, built ten years earlier on the opposite side of the square. Excavations beneath the Basilica built by Augustus brought to light remains of this earlier building and of part of the atrium of a private house, almost certainly the one that the ancient sources record as belonging to Scipio Africanus and that

Sempronius Gracchus acquired with public money after his death. The building constructed by Augustus is the largest basilica documented in the Forum as it occupies a space 101 metres long and 49 metres wide; unfortunately, the utilisation of this monument as a quarry for building material over the centuries does not permit a detailed knowledge of its original appearance. Its grandeur is however perceptible from the view that the visitor has from the east side along the street that separates it from the Temple of the Dioscures

(entrance into the Basilica is not allowed). The interior, divided into five aisles by brick pillars faced in marble and adorned with a pavement of marble slabs, provided accommodated various civil tribunals that, according to contemporary evidence, were all able to function at the same time, separated by massive curtains suspended from the ceiling. The central nave, wider than the four side aisles, was three-storeys; large windows opened onto the top storey to light the hall. The best conserved part of the building is that towards the Forum, which includes

38. *Aerial view of the Horrea Agrippiana and of the Hall in opus latericium belonging to the Athenaeum*

39. *Horrea Agrippiana*

the entrance stairs made, in response to the slope of the ground at this point, of seven marble steps on the east side and of only one step on the west side. Nearly in the centre of the facade, where the main entrance to the building was, at the point where a pilaster adorned with a Doric half-column has been almost entirely reconstructed, two pairs of statue bases are visible, completely inscribed. Both of the two larger bases supported statues carried here from another site, perhaps saved from the sack of Alaric (the name of the man who undertook this re-installation

was Gabinius Vetius Praetestatus, praefect of the city in A.D. 416), whereas the inscriptions on the two smaller bases, datable to the III century A.D., and now placed on top of the bases of Vetius Praetestatus, belonged to works of the famous Greek sculptors of the Classical period, Polyclitus and Timarchus. Many of the steps of the stairway, especially on the east, have coarse engravings: these are *tabulae lusoriae*, boards for games of skill and dexterity, used by the boys, loungers, and idlers who, as the ancient sources record, crowded into the

Forum every hours of day and night. Before reaching the Temple of the Castores ㊴, that closes the side along the south of the Forum square, we cross a street of basalt blocks, the *vicus Tuscus*, from the name of the inhabitants of Etruscan origin who once resided there. The large brick buildings along the left side of the street form a complex of **Domitianic buildings**, in part occupied in the VI century A.D. by the Church of **S. Maria Antiqua** ㊱, adorned with valuable paintings of the Byzantine period but now not open to

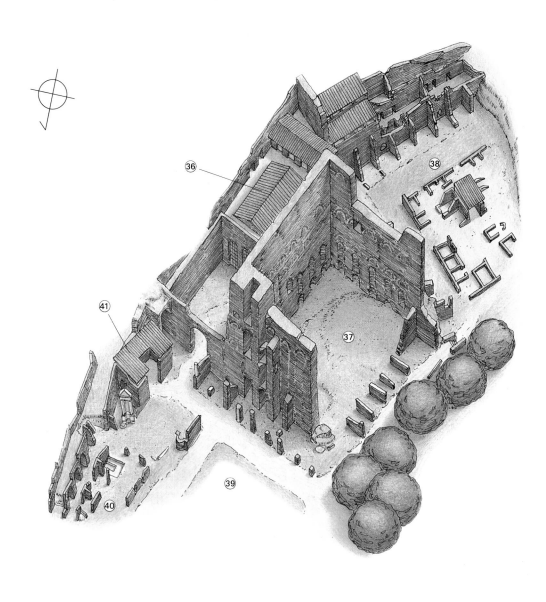

36 S. Maria Antiqua

37 Hall in opus latericium

38 *Horrea Agrippiana*

39 Temple of the Castores

40 *Lacus Iuturnae*

41 Oratory of the Forty Martyrs

visitors. The only visible building is a large **hall in opus latericium** (the so-called Temple of Augustus) ㊲. This hall, preceded on the *vicus Tuscus* side by a row of shops of the Hadrianic period, and on the Forum side by a portico, originally had a vaulted roof and marble revetment on the walls, articulated by large niches. The entirety of these buildings, that date in their first phase to the end of the I century A.D., could correspond to the *Athenaeum*, the building destined by Hadrian to scholarship. This identification could also explain the presence of the niches that could have been used in this case to hold books. The name that the complex took on, the *Athenaeum*, could refer to a site of the cult of Minerva (the patron goddess of scholarship) that already existed on this site. If so, it could be the sanctuary of Minerva where, from the Domitianic period onwards, military diplomas with the names of the soldiers dismissed with honours were fixed which the ancient sources noted near the Temple of Augustus, situated in the Velabrum a short distance from this point, in the area behind the Basilica Julia. Behind the Domitianic buildings just described, are found a group of rooms placed around a large courtyard; they belonged to a storehouse, identified by an inscription found within, with the *Horrea Agrippiana* ㊳, built in the last years of the I century B.C. by Augustus' son-in-law, Agrippa.

The Temple of the Dioscures, also designated by the Romans as the **Temple of the Castores** ㊴, is one of the most well-known symbols of ancient Rome in the world. Only the three large Corinthian columns and the architrave set on top of them, in the centre of the long east side, are preserved; they belong to the Augustan phase of the Temple which was rebuilt by the initiative of Tiberius in A.D. 6. This restoration is the last testified building project in this building. The temple had in fact been vowed by the dictator Aulus Postumius Albinus in memory of the prodigious apparition of the Dioscuri in the Forum, as heralds of the Roman victory over the Latins in the battle at Lake Regillus in 499 B.C.; the dedication of the temple on the 27 of January, 484 B.C. was presided over by the son of the dictator, who had died in the meantime. Remains of the original decoration (now displayed in room IV of the Antiquarium Forense) were found in the vicinity, especially during excavations in the area of the Basilica Julia, beneath the remains of the house of Scipio Africanus. Important restorations were undertaken in 117 B.C. by the consul Quintus Caecilius Metellus Dalmaticus, and in 74 B.C. during the urban praetorship of Verres; he, as Cicero presents in detail, found a way to amass a large amount of money by putting out on contract work that was actually useless. The large podium of opus caementicium dates to the restoration of Metellus, while the tuff blocks, covered by a modern roof, placed along the side of the temple visible from the *vicus Tuscus*, are the only remains of the original podium. On both the long sides, the podium is interrupted by a succession of square rooms recognisable as the bankers' shops which the ancient sources recorded within the temple. The building also functioned as a political meeting place; during the Republican period, the Senate used to meet here often and many judiciary activities took place in the immediate vicinity, where the Rostra, the tribunes used by magistrates and orators, stood.

Divided from the Temple of the Castores by a narrow street made of blocks of

40. The three surviving columns of the Temple of the Castores

41. The Lacus Iuturnae; the brick substructures of the Domus Tiberiana stand in the background

The cults of the Forum: the Dioscures

The Greek cult of the *Dioscuri* (literally 'the sons of Zeus') was introduced very early in Rome and Latium and can be documented with certainty at least from the second half of the VI century B.C., the period to which is dated the important bronze plaque dedicated to the divine twins Castor and Pollux, inscribed in Archaic Latin, found at Lavinius in 1958. This might explain why, at the beginning of the V century B.C., it was possible to build a temple in their honour within the Forum, that is to say inside the pomerium, the sacred line that marked the boundary of the city, within which, according to the strict rules of Roman religion, it was not possible to house a foreign cult. Among the multiple functions of the

basalt stands an area in which are concentrated structures from different periods; they constitute the monumental area around the spring consecrated to Juturna, the *Lacus Iuturnae* ㊵. The cult of the nymph, sister of Turnus, king of the Ruteli, was probably introduced by Lavinius, together with the cult of the *Dioscuri*, at the end of the Archaic period. A recent study based on the results of excavations in this area has clarified the earliest monumental phase of the complex. The point where the spring gushed out, one of the few existing inside the city and perhaps endowed with healthy properties, was defined by a basin (*lacus*) in the first half of the II century B.C. Behind this first systemisation was probably Lucius Aemilius Paullus, the same person who placed in this area two marble statues of the Dioscures in Archaising style (now displayed in a section of the Antiquarium Forense not yet open to the public), to commemorate their second appearance at the spring, when they announced to the city Lucius Aemilius Paullus' victory over Perseus in the battle of Pydna (168 B.C.). A few years later, during the work undertaken by Quintus Cecilius Metellus Dalmaticus in the nearby Temple of the Castores, the basin was partially rebuilt, and a rectangular base to support the group of the *Dioscuri* was placed in the centre of it. The present appearance of the *lacus*, lined with marble slabs, dates to the Trajanic period, when the entire area was extensively restored. On the south side of the basin's edge is preserved a plaster cast of a marble altar; it was found inside the basin together with the remains of the statues of the Dioscures. The lateral faces of the altar are decorated with reliefs representing the Dioscures, Leda, Jupiter and perhaps Helen. In front of the basin, on the side bordering the House of the Vestal Virgins ㊼, was found a large room with a cross vaulted ceiling and niches along the walls (in one of these was perhaps the statue of Aesculapius, now displayed in the entrance to the Antiquarium Forense). To the south of this room is found the Sacellum of Juturna, composed of an aedicula (small shrine) on a high podium with columns and tympanum of marble which dates to the II century A.D.; as the inscription on the re-used block that formed the architrave states, here was the true cult site of the nymph, whose statue was placed on a podium also revetted in marble. The position of the small shrine is strongly oblique with respect to the other parts of the complex; the reason for this divergence is that the rebuilding of the little shrine followed the earlier orientation of the whole area, known from the remains of other buildings found beneath those now visible which pre-date the

destruction caused by the Neronian fire of A.D. 64. Plaster casts of some decorative elements found within this complex, have been placed in front of the small shrine: an altar adorned on the front with two figures (Turnus and Juturna or, according to another hypothesis, Mars and Venus) and a marble well-head inscribed on its rim with the name of the dedicator, *M. Barbatius Pollio*, curule aedile in the last years of the I century B.C. Abundant material connected with the cult was found during excavations in this area, precious evidence of the long patronage of this sacred complex. From one of the rooms next to the sacellum came the base of a statue dedicated to Constantine by an important man in Rome of the first half of the IV century A.D., *Flavius Maesius Egnatius*, who was *curator acquarum* (responsible for the city' s aqueducts); he is said to have moved the offices connected with his position from the Campus Martius to the *Lacus Iuturnae*. According to some scholars these offices correspond to the rooms along the boundary wall of the House of the Vestal Virgins. Behind the Sacellum of Juturna, a vast area was occupied by a Christian

Dioscures as healers, helpers and protectors of horsemen, their double function as helpers in battles and announcers of victory prevailed at Rome with the dedication of their temple in the Forum. On 15 July, the *dies natalis* of the Temple, coinciding with the date of the battle of Lake Regillus, a procession of horsemen took place near the sacred building. The horsemen wore purple mantles with scarlet stripes like those worn by the Dioscuri when they appeared near the river Sagra during the battle between the Crotoniates and the Locrenses; the parade horses were all white, like the horses of the Dioscures.

42. Aedicula of Juturna

43. Head of the horse of one of the Dioscures from the Lacus Iuturnae

building, called the **Oratory of the Forty Martyrs** ㊶ after the large painting that adorned the apse: the devotion bestowed on the forty soldiers of Diocletian, sentenced to freeze to death in the cold waters of a pond, documents the Christianisation of the most ancient cult of the nymph of the spring.

44. Marble altar with a depiction of Turnus and Juturna

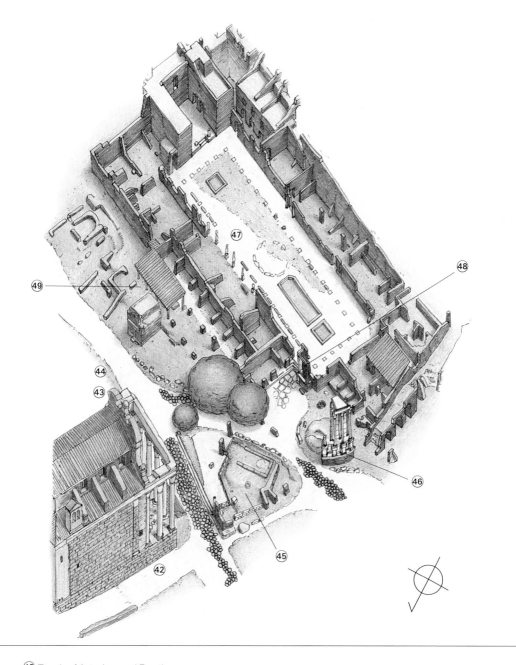

42 Temple of Antoninus and Faustina
43 Cemetery
44 Private house
45 *Regia*
46 Temple of Vesta
47 House of the Vestal Virgins
48 Aedicula
49 *Domus Publica*

THE AREA OF THE REGIA:
FROM THE TEMPLE OF ANTONINUS AND FAUSTINA
TO THE DOMUS PUBLICA

Proceeding along the ancient street that leads to the Arch of Titus ⑤①, constructed on the north slopes of the Palatine, the first imposing building on the left is the **Temple of Antoninus and Faustina** ㊷. The excellent state of preservation of the monument is due to its transformation into the Church of S. Lorenzo in Miranda, that from the VII to the VIII century occupied its cella. The large inscription carved on the architrave of the pronaos, which has six columns in the facade with cipollino shafts and Corinthian white marble capitals and with two other columns on the long sides, records that the temple was dedicated by the Senate to the deified Imperial couple; actually, it is a new dedication, since the building was erected in A.D. 141 by Antoninus Pius in memory of his wife. In front of the temple is a modern brick staircase which encases the podium in opus latericium of the altar, whereas the lower part of a marble statue found during the excavations has been placed in the middle of the pronaos. The podium and the cella were in opus quadrata of peperino faced with marble; all the slabs were removed during the recovery of precious building materials from the Forum at the beginning of the 1500s. The labour of the workers in that period is particularly recognisable in the deep holes in the joints of the blocks of peperino where the marble slabs were fixed with metal cramps. The building, however, ran the risk of being completely dismantled like many others in the immediate vicinity; in fact, the deep furrows visible on the upper part of the column shafts have been interpreted as the traces of ropes used during an attempt, fortunately unsuccessful, to make them collapse so that they could be reused. Of the original architectural decoration of the temple, the frieze that decorated the architrave on the long sides is

45. View from above of the Cemetery near the Temple of Antoninus and Faustina during the period of the excavations of G. Boni

preserved, with pairs of heraldic griffins flanked on the sides by volute candelabra. Immediately to the east of the pronaos of the Temple of Antoninus and Faustina, one can note an area with flower-beds of different sizes and shapes, that repeat the form of the tombs discovered during the excavations of the beginning of our century and belonging to a **Cemetery** ㊸ of the Iron Age period (X-VIII century B.C.). Probably, this most ancient necropolis was related to an inhabited site of the same period on the slopes and above on the hills around the Forum valley (Palatine, Velia, Capitol). For the most part, the tombs were for cremation burials, but in the course of time inhumation burials make their appearance. Generalised use of the cemetery stopped in the middle of the VIII century B.C., contemporary with the traditional date of the foundation of the city; from that time on the necropolis only received children's tombs, until it was definitively abandoned in the VII century B.C. The most significant funerary equipment from those tombs can be admired in rooms I and II on the ground floor of the Antiquarium Forense. Three little rooms near the sepulchral area, subterranean compared with the Augustan level of the via Sacra at this point, were considered, for a long time, part of a brothel, but should be recognised as service rooms of a **private house** ㊹, perhaps intended for slaves' quarters, as in the case of a similar arrangement visible under the House of

46. *The Regia during the excavations; the circular altar dedicated to Mars is visible on the left*

47. *Fragment of Bucchero ware with the graffito 'REX', now preserved in the Epigraphy Department of the Museo Nazionale Romano*

48. *Terracotta architectural revetment depicting the Minotaur and a panther which was found near the Regia*

Marcus Aemilius Scaurus ⑤⑤, excavated on the north-east slopes of the Palatine.
In front of the Temple of Antoninus and Faustina, there is a building whose origins date to the most ancient period of the life of the city, unfortunately now in terrible condition as a result of the Renaissance plunder. It is the *Regia* ④⑤, a part of the great palace complex of the kings, which extended as far as the Temple of Romulus ⑤⓪. From the beginning of the Republic, the building was used for the duties related to the sacerdotal offices of the *rex sacrorum* and the *pontifex maximus*, who after the expulsion of the kings supervised the offices of the official cult of the city. Many studies have been made of this small building, and certainly the attempt to understand more and more of the most ancient political centre of Rome will continue to stimulate research for a long time. The results that have emerged to date from excavation, during which a vase fragment bearing the

word *rex* carved came to light, have at any rate clarified the history of the building phases of the *Regia*. The phase of the building actually visible dates to the repair undertaken by Domitius Calvinus in 36 B.C., which followed faithfully a much earlier arrangement, datable perhaps to the last years of the Etruscan monarchy (around 525 B.C.). In turn, the Archaic phase of the *Regia* was preceded by other building operations, that began with the construction of a cluster of huts, whose plan is very similar to the Iron Age ash-urns found in the 'pozzo' tombs of the nearby Cemetery ④③. A terracotta slab representing a man with bull-like head identified as the Minotaur belongs to the decoration of the Archaic phase of the *Regia*. Proceeding from the

Regia's western outer perimeter (turned therefore towards the back of the Temple of Divus Julius), noteworthy, almost in the centre, is a rather narrow, square room, defined by tuff walls of opus reticulatum; on the top of the south wall are visible the remains of an inscription which indicates that this room was used by the heralds of the pontifices and flamines (*calatores*). looking out over the balustrade that marks the boundary of the south side of the *Regia*, where several fragments of the marble decoration of the late Republican phase are piled up, it is possible to see three rooms of unequal size; they are supposed to be, from the left side: the Shrine of Mars, with a large circular altar where Numa put the spears and shields of Mars; a central room with no clear use, and lastly on the right side the

room identified with the Shrine of *Ops*, the goddess of plenty. This cluster of rooms opened on a trapezoidal courtyard with a double arcade, now barely recognisable. It is clear that the two main rooms consecrated the double duty of the king, one as a warrior, the other as the guardian of the community's wealth. In addition to the sacred objects already mentioned, in the Regia were preserved or displayed some of the most important political and religious documents of the town, like the public archives, the annals on which were written the principle events as well as the calendar which regulated year by year the religious life of the entire community. Like the *Regia*, the building devoted to the cult of Vesta, the *Atrium Vestae*, also had several building periods, in that it dates back to the most ancient period of occupation of the area near the Forum, when it was in fact an integrated part of the royal residence. The worship of Vesta, associated with the care of an eternal fire, was the symbol of the hearth burning in the royal residence; with the birth of the Republic, it became the communal hearth of all the citizens (like the hearth of Hestia in the prytaneum of the Greek cities) and its continuous nourishment was committed to the corporation of the Vestals. The entire complex

49. The round Temple of Vesta

50 The Aedicula in front of the entrance to the House of the Vestals

The shields of Mars and the priesthood of the Salii

The bronze shields kept with the spear of Mars in the sacrarium of the *Regia* were considered in antiquity to be the first of the seven talismans of the greatness of Rome and of its empire. Their origin is connected to a prodigious event, which was dated to the pious Numa Pompilius, successor to Romulus in the leadership of the city. The story, as recounted by Plutarch (*The life of Numa*, 13) is the following. During a

consists of the temple of the goddess and the residence of the priestesses, closely linked together. The *Temple of Vesta* ⑭, with a characteristic round shape, was destroyed more than once by fires that broke out because of the fire which, within, was so carefully preserved. The remains now visible belong to the reconstruction undertaken by the wife of Emperor Septimius Severus, Julia Domna, after the fire of A.D. 191. The form of the temple

belongs to its radical recomposition after the Neronian fire of A.D. 64, which changed the orientation of the entire area of the House of the Vestal Virgins (or *Atrium Vestae*), by aligning it on the major axis of the Forum (a few remains of the earlier reconstruction of the Republican period are visible in the west end of the House of the Vestal Virgins). The part of the Temple facing the Forum was rebuilt with abundant modern additions

in travertine facing a circular core in opus caementicium. There was no statue of the deity within the Temple, as was normally the custom, since in this case she was symbolised by the perpetual fire burning on the altar. Ancient sources however, record the existence of a recess called the *penus Vestae*, the most secret place in the entire building, accessible only to the Vestals and in which ancient objects of special veneration and antiquity were

serious plague a figure-eight bronze shields (*ancile*) fell from the sky into the hands of the king and shortly thereafter the epidemic ended. Numa learned from the nymph Egeria and the Muses that the shield had appeared for the salvation of Rome. Therefore Numa

ordered a blacksmith named Veturius Mamurius to make another eleven shields identical to the first one; the blacksmith succeeded so well in following the order that not even the king himself was able to recognise the original shield. Since that time, the custody of the

twelve shields (*ancilia*) was given in custody to the priests of Mars, named Salii, for the 'jumping' war dance that they performed in March and in October, in correspondence with the ceremonies that indicated the opening and closure of war season. The dance

was composed of three elements following the same rhythm: songs, steps (two short jumps on the same foot and a third one as long as the first two on the other foot) and the sound of the spears hit on the shields.

preserved. These included the Palladium, the small image of Minerva which, according to tradition, Aeneas had saved from Troy and brought with him to Latium, a sacred token of the universal dominion promised to Rome. To the right of the entrance to the **House of the Vestal Virgins** (47), which can be reached by a ramp which passes over the Republican remains of the *Atrium Vestae*, is found an **aedicula** (48). This contains part of one of the two marble Ionic columns which adorned the front. An inscription on the architrave records that the monument was built with public money by the will of the Senate and the Roman people. The function of this small religious building is uncertain; it may have been a *compitum*, a sanctuary placed at cross-roads, places considered to be exposed to the influence of underworld gods and therefore requiring protection (in fact, the via Sacra intersects a small road, the *vicus Vestae*, in front of the House of the Vestals). The House of the Vestal Virgins, restored several times between the time of Nero and that of Septimius Severus, was built round a courtyard or atrium surrounded by marble colonnades on four sides, with pools in the centre, one of which was

subsequently transformed into a kind of octagonal flower-bed. The rooms on the south side, in front of the entrance, on the basis of the objects found within have been identified as a bakery, a small flour-mill and a kitchen. A flight of steps in the middle of the marble colonnade led to the upper floor, where the rooms in which the Vestals lived were probably located, as well as several baths heated by stove pipes within the walls. A second flight of stairs, on the west end, passes over an apsidal area, in which it is possible to recognise the reconstruction of an ancient cult site sacred to *Aius Locutius*, a little known god in the pantheon of Roman deities, to whom Cicero records a small sanctuary was dedicated in this area. A large room opens onto the east colonnade that in turn has three rooms facing onto it on each side. This room, usually defined as the tablinum, was certainly the most important residential area of the entire complex. The north colonnade of the courtyard is occupied almost entirely by marble bases, on which some of the female statues, found during the excavations, have been placed. The women here depicted are completely covered by ample robes and represented in a stance suited

to the virginity of the Vestals. The statues in fact, represent the Head Priestesses of the religious order, to whom the inscriptions on the marble bases, praising their virtues and their extreme dedication to their holy duties, refer. All the inscriptions belong to the last period during which the House of the Vestals was used between the time of Septimius Severus and Theodosius. On one of them, the name of the High Priestess was erased in antiquity: it has been supposed to be the statue of Claudia, the Vestal Virgin who left her priesthood to become a Christian at the end of the IV century A.D. The group of rooms on the west side is not well preserved. The ruins of the plan of the House of the Vestals of the Republican period visible from here are however of great interest; this earlier phase, as mentioned of the nearby Temple of Vesta, had a different orientation from the remains visible today. Six rooms were partially restored (one for each of the Vestals) and face onto a courtyard where in some places the original paving survives: a tessellatum with inserts of coloured stone, which belongs to a type of floor decoration in vogue between the second half of the II and beginning

The Vestal Virgins

The *sacerdotes Vestales*, who were six in number, ministered to the cult of Vesta, the Roman deity of the domestic hearth. At the beginning of the Republican era, this religious order, the only female priesthood in ancient Rome, replaced the daughters of royal dynasty, who were originally entrusted with guarding the domestic hearth of the house of the king. The Vestal Virgins were chosen by the Pontifex Maximus (*captio*) from a group of twenty free-born young girls between the ages of six and ten, free of physical imperfections, whose parents were alive. The Vestals, whose hair was cut and hung on a lotus tree during the course of the *captio*, were also distinguished by special dress (a white veil that also covered the shoulders, the *suffibulum*, and a kind of woollen fillet resembling a diadem divided into six bands, the *infula*. They served for thirty years during which time they were required to maintain their chastity, but once dismissed from the cult (*exauguratio*) they were able to marry as well. The violation of their vow of chastity was punishable by the burial alive of the guilty Vestal in the *Campus Sceleratus* (field of villains), near the Porta Collina on the Quirinal Hill, while the punishment for her accomplice was death by whipping in the Comitium. The Vestals enjoyed many privileges, first of all, emancipation from paternal authority which was, however, in part assumed by the Pontifex Maximus, to whom they were bound by symbolic marriage. Special places were reserved for them at gladiatorial games and theatres and they had the right to be buried in a tomb, perhaps communal, within the city walls; a condemned criminal could be reprieved if he passed a Vestal in the street on the day of his execution. The most important of the Vestal's duties was to watch over the sacred fire burning in the Temple, which must never go out. If this ever happened the negligent Vestal was whipped by the Pontifex Maximus and the fire was rekindled by rubbing together pieces of wood. During the period of the *Vestalia* (7 to 15 June) the Temple was opened, ritually cleansed and made accessible only to women, while the millstone for the flour used for the special salt cakes prepared by the Vestals (*mola salsa*) and the donkey, whose braying had saved the Goddess from the clutches of Priapus, were decorated with wreaths.

51. Statue of a Vestal

of the I centuries B.C. Leaving the House of the Vestal Virgins and turning right onto a narrow street parallel to the via Sacra it is possible to reach the remains of the **Domus Publica** ⑲, protected by a modern roof. This was the residence of the Pontifex Maximus, who lived there continually from the pontificate of Cornelius Scipius Nasica Corculus (153 B.C.) to that of Marcus Aemilius Lepidus, who died in 12 B.C.; Caesar lived here from 62 B.C. (the year in which his pontificate began) down to the day on which he was murdered on the 15th of March in 44 B.C.). Precisely to the Caesarean period are assigned several areas protected by roofing: a colonnade, of which the stylobate survives with the remains of a travertine half-column and a small moulding of the same stone, and the apsidal room decorated with mosaic paving, identified with a bathing area. Also belonging to the late Republican period is a room with a floor of opus signinum, decorated with diamond-shaped tiles set into a meander pattern. Another room, with marble paving and wall paintings of landscapes in the so-called "third style", dates to the Augustan era. As can be seen, these diverse elements do not provide a very clear idea of this building, one of the most important in Ancient Rome

until the Augustan age, when the Princeps transferred the headquarters of the Pontifex Maximus to his residence on the Palatine, ceding the original building to the Vestal Virgins. More precise information on the structure and history of the *Domus Publica* must await the conclusion of the excavations in the area of the building situated behind the covered rooms that is currently sealed off by a fence.

52. House of the Vestal Virgins, north portico with statues of the Head Vestal Virgins

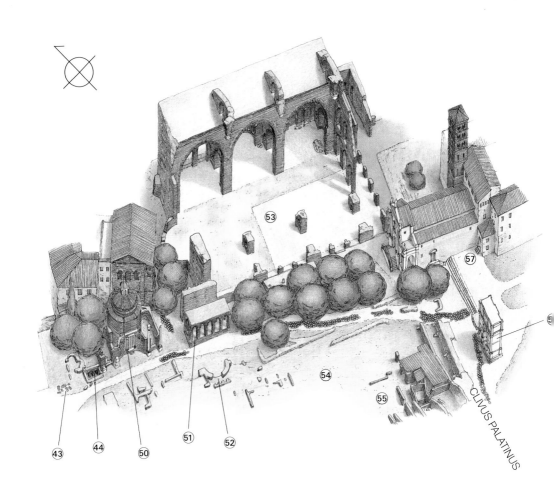

CLIVUS PALATINUS

43 Cemetery
44 Private house
50 Temple of Romulus
51 Mediaeval arcade
52 Sacellum of Bacchus

53 Basilica of Maxentius
54 *Horrea Vespasiani*
55 House of M. Aemilius Scaurus
56 Arch of Titus
57 Antiquarium Forense

BETWEEN THE PALATINE AND THE VELIA: FROM THE TEMPLE OF ROMULUS TO THE ARCH OF TITUS

In correspondence to the so-called Temple of Romulus ⑤⓪, the road onto which all of the buildings on the north side of the Forum face rises more steeply, ascending a saddle between the hills of the Palatine to the right and the Velia to the left. According to the district division (*regiones*) that date to the age of Augustus, the entire section between the Basilica Fulvia-Aemilia ⑤ and the Temple of Venus and Rome which faces onto the valley of the Colosseum, belonged not to *Regio* VIII (*Forum Romanum*) but to *Regio* IV (*Templum Pacis*, named after the Forum built by Vespasian), whereas the buildings located on the opposite side of the road, starting from the House of the Vestals ㊼, were part of *Regio* X (*Palatinum*). Not only ancient topography shows that from this point onwards we are outside the area of the Forum proper; with a simple glance, it is possible to note that, with rare exceptions, primarily private houses or utilitarian buildings (such as warehouses and offices of the Imperial bureaucracy) are found in this part of the itinerary, in strong contrast to the

sumptuousness of the commemorative monuments of the Forum square.

The *Temple of Romulus* ⑤⓪, a round sacred building, that has survived almost intact as a result of its conversion in the mid VI century A.D. into the vestibule of the Church dedicated to Sts. Cosmas and Damian, is generally thought to be a monument built in memory of the Emperor Maxentius' son, who died in boyhood in the first years of the IV century A.D. The entrance to the temple is at a much higher level than the road, revealing its foundations, two small drainage pipes with a triangular cover and the remains of a Mediaeval burial area delimited by terracotta slabs. The exposure of part of the foundation, visible also in other monuments in the area ⑤② ⑤③ ⑤⑥, is due to the fact that the road brought to light in 1899 reached the Augustan level thereby dismantling the road built

after the fire of A.D. 64 onto which opened all of the buildings constructed after that date. The facade of the temple, that assumed the concave shape now visible following a partial rebuilding carried out during the reign of Constantine, contains a pair of niches for statues on either side of the entrance (later walled-up). To the far east and west open two apsidal rooms, with independent entrances from the road, framed by cipollino marble columns standing on high plinths of Carrara marble; these two side rooms communicated directly with the central apsidal room through two open doors on the long sides. While there is no trace left of the marble that faced the brick walls, the bronze door, set in a marble frame and flanked by two porphyry columns (the preferred stone for Imperial buildings of the late Antique period) supporting a richly decorated re-used marble

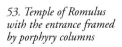

53. Temple of Romulus with the entrance framed by porphyry columns

architrave with a floral design, has been preserved. As mentioned earlier, it is generally thought, on the basis of Mediaeval sources, that the temple was dedicated to the son of Maxentius. Recently, however, serious doubts have been expressed over this identification and some historians have proposed that the Temple of Jupiter Stator was located here. The temple was a simple precinct built at the time of the foundation of the city (at the point where the Roman soldiers, put to flight by the Sabines, stopped and turned back to renew battle after Romulus had invoked the god), that was converted into a proper temple in 294

B.C. as decreed by the Senate. It is possible that the building dedicated to Maxentius' son may have replaced the older construction for a short while until, after the victory of Constantine, the ancient cult was revived in its original position and associated with that of the Penates. The images of these gods may have been housed in the two rooms on either side of the apsidal room, as the temple dedicated to their worship on the Velia had been demolished by the Basilica of Maxentius ⑤③. On the right side of the road, in front of a **Mediaeval brick arcade** ⑤①, a large hemicycle, also constructed in *opus*

latericium, can be seen. Since its discovery it has been recognised as the **Sacellum of Bacchus** ⑤②, mentioned in an epigram of Martial and recognisable through the record of its form preserved on a coin minted in the time of Antoninus Pius. According to the image on the coin, the hemicycle encircled a small round temple within which a statue stood. A fragment of a curvilinear architrave (now housed in a closed section of the Antiquarium Forense) is considered part of the architectural decoration of the Sacellum; the inscription refers to the restoration of the building by Antoninus Pius, while the relief with a dancing Maenad framing the surviving part of the inscription proves that the architrave belonged to the Sacellum of Bacchus (a reproduction of the fragment is visible a little beyond the hemicycle, near the large laurel bushes). The summit of the Velia hill is completely occupied by the gigantic brick construction of the **Basilica of Maxentius** ⑤③ or of Constantine, one of the most impressive buildings of the late Antique period visible in Rome. The construction of this Basilica not only resulted in the transfer of the Temple of the Penates, but it also demolished an area occupied by the State warehouses (the

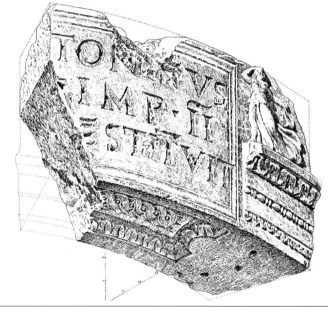

54. Fragment of an architrave with a dancing Maenad and inscription of Antoninus Pius which belongs to the Sacellum of Bacchus

The Penates

The worship of the Penates, whose name expresses their nature as household gods, who watched over the family storeroom (*penus*) is strictly linked to the domestic hearth and, therefore, to Vesta and the

Lares. Originally a cult connected to the individual and to the king's home, at the beginning of the Republic it assumed a public character from whence derives the well-known epithet, *Penates Publici*. The temple dedicated to these deities, who are thought to have

been introduced into Latium by Aeneas, was situated on the Velia not far from the Forum (Dionysius of Halicarnassus, I, 68, 1), more or less in correspondence with the west apse of the Basilica of Maxentius, the building of which resulted in the destruction of the temple.

Horrea Piperataria, for the conservation of spices) and by private houses (in one of these houses of the II century A.D. the famous Greek doctor, Galen, lived). Initially built by Maxentius, improved under Constantine and finally partially reconstructed at the end of the IV century A.D., the basilica has two entrances, one on the east side (near the front of the Church of S. Maria Nova, better known as S. Francesca Romana), composed of a vestibule onto which three doors opened, and the other, accessible from the road leading out of the Forum, built at the end of the IV century A.D. The appearance of this entrance, now lost, was much more monumental than the one belonging to the first phase of the building, as it was formed by an avant-corps supported by four porphyry columns. The interior was divided into three aisles, with the central one, larger than the lateral ones, articulated by tall columns of proconnesian marble, all lost with the exception of the one that was placed by Pope Paul V in the square in front of S. Maria Maggiore in 1613 (14.5 metres high). The best preserved part of the interior of the building is that corresponding to the north aisle, divided into three

This is the reason that worship of the Penates took place thereafter in the two apsidal rooms that flanked the central space of the Temple of Romulus, also built by Maxentius on the nearest site available to the destroyed Temple of the Penates. Significantly, when in A.D. 527 Pope Felix IV made a Church out of the hall of the Forum of Peace near the rear wall of the Rotunda of the Temple of Romulus, he dedicated it to Sts. Cosmas and Damian, whose religious sphere is very similar to that of the Penates.

55. Basilica of Maxentius

56. North aisle of the Basilica of Maxentius; in the centre stands the apsidal room partially rebuilt at the end of the IV century A.D.

communicating areas and still covered by a vault with a coffered ceiling. At the far end of the central area is an apse, originally closed off by a gate which was not part of the original project but that, like the south entrance, belongs to the later reconstruction of the building. Still surviving from the first phase of the building, however, is the apse which closed off the central nave to the west, placed on axis with the most important of the three original entrances. Here stood the statue of Maxentius, replaced after death of the emperor at the Battle of Ponte Milvio (A.D. 312) by that of his victorious opponent, Constantine. The statue was a colossus with bronze body and marble head, arms and legs; fragments of marble parts (head and part of arms) are now exhibited in the courtyard of Palazzo dei Conservatori on the Capitol. The head displays the unnaturally rigid features of the Emperor, dominated by deep-set eyes. The Basilica of Maxentius has recently been identified as the headquarters of the City Praefecture, the most important administrative office of the city in the late Antique period, whose most senior officers left a record of their activities in the

reconstruction of many buildings in the Forum. In the IV century, the *Secretarium Senatus* may have been transferred here from the Curia Julia and in particular to the apse in the central area of the north aisle; the court was used for trials of Senate members, which were held behind closed doors from then on. On the other side of the road, the area in front of the Basilica of Maxentius was occupied in the Imperial period by warehouses, of which only the supporting pillars with concrete centre faced in bricks survive. Recent excavations have dated the early foundations to the years immediately after the Neronian fire and identified them as the *Horrea Vespasiani* ⑤④, used in part as the fish market, substantiated by the discovery of several basins and abundant remains of shells in the drainage pipes. Subsequently, from the Hadrianic period, it seems that the complex was used as the headquarters of the Imperial administration. The later building works to seen in the area date to the V-VI centuries A.D. At the far end of this section, almost in front of the Arch of Titus, a modern shed protects the remains of a private house belonging to the late

Republican age, identified as the **House of Marcus Aemilius Scaurus** ⑤⑤. Some details of its building history are known. Constructed beginning in 74 B.C. by Marcus Aemilius Scaurus, in 58 B.C., the year in which the owner held the office of aedile, the house was embellished with four of the 360 Phrygian marble columns that, according to Pliny, he had erected to decorate a temporary theatre. A few years later, in 53 B.C., Scaurus sold the house to Publius Clodius for about fifteen million sesterces. This tribune of the people, like Scaurus before him, used to receive every day in the atrium a throng of people, bound to him by the strong ties of the patron-client system. The day he was murdered by Milone, it was to this part of the house that a great part of the Roman people flocked to pay homage to his body. Around 17 B.C., the famous columns in the courtyard were used to decorate the stage of the Theatre of Marcellus. The latest mention of the house before the Neronian fire dates to the first half of the I century A.D., the house was purchased by Gaius Cecina Largus, as an extension to his own house. Archaeologists have also discovered an underground section of the house which includes a small room occupied by a household shrine dedicated to the Lares (*lararium*) and some rooms built in opus reticulatum; these rooms, very small, with the simplest of mosaic floors made of Travertine chips, were the slaves quarters. Other rooms, decorated with black and white mosaic pavements, were instead connected with the thermal baths. This is the only house still visible in the densely populated area that one stretched from here to the *Domus Publica* from the Archaic period to the early Imperial age (Cicero's house was, in fact, adjacent to the residence of the Pontifex Maximus). In fact, excavations carried out in recent years in this area have brought to light some houses built around 520 B.C. and already organised around an atrium complete with an impluvium and provided with a small garden; these houses were reconstructed several times between the III and I centuries B.C. Almost the entire space between the Basilica of Maxentius and the

Arch of Titus is occupied by an imposing staircase leading to the Temple of Venus and Rome, that housed from the High Middle Ages the convent of S. Maria Nova (today the site of the offices of the Archaeological Superintendency of Rome and of the Antiquarium Forense). The section of basalt paving that ends in front of the staircase, on a different axis with respect to the road on which we have walked along until now, represents the only surviving remains of the road of the post-Neronian period, dismantled during the excavations. It is onto this street, much more regular than that of the Augustan age, that most of the buildings constructed on the slopes of the Palatine and the Velia, including the **Arch of Titus** 56, face. As the inscription legible on the attic of the Arch on the Colosseum side records, it was built in memory of the emperor, after his death in A.D. 81, by the Senate and the Roman people. The survival of the monument is

also due in this case to its reuse in the Middle Ages, when the mighty pillars were inserted into the fortifications of the Frangipane family and a small room was created within the barrel-vault. The massive damage this use caused was repaired by Giuseppe Valadier in 1822, under Pope Pius VII, with travertine additions (the commemorative inscription relating to this restoration can be seen on the attic facing the Forum). The arch with a single passage, still retains most of the external decoration on the side facing the Colosseum. The façade is articulated by four composite marble half-columns; a frieze above the architrave shows the official triumphal procession for the victory over the Jews, celebrated by Vespasian and Titus in A.D. 71. The archivault is decorated with two winged Victories bearing standards, while the keystone is adorned with an image of the Goddess Rome (the one on the opposite side instead, features the Genius of the Roman People). However, the most

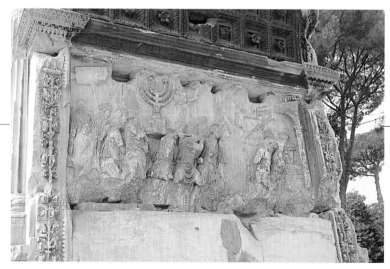

remarkable decoration of the monument is positioned inside the arch. The ceiling in fact, with its magnificent coffered vault, depicts in the centre a representation of Titus transported into the heavens by an eagle (an allusion to his deification after death), whilst on the sides of the passageway there are panels illustrating the most important moments of the triumph over the Jewish people. Looking in the direction of the Forum, the left panel displays a group of bearers carrying silver trumpets and a candelabrum with seven arms, the most important objects of the booty plundered during the conquest of Jerusalem; near them are visible other servants carrying signs on which the names of the conquered cities may have been written. On the far right of the panel is an arch surmounted by two quadrigae (four-horse chariots): it represents the Porta Triumphalis, located in the Forum Boarium, from which the triumphal ceremony began. In the centre of the right-hand panel appears Titus standing on a quadriga, preceded by the goddess Roma (or *Virtus*), who leads the horses with the bit; behind the emperor are found a Victory and two male figures, a young man with a naked torso and an older man dressed in a toga, identified respectively as personifications of the People and Senate of Rome. In the background are depicted profiles of heads and many lictors' fasces represented in a disorderly manner to convey an idea of the crowd of magistrates who followed the triumphant emperor. From the Arch of Titus the ancient road turns right, sloping steeply, and takes the name of *Clivus Palatinus*. The visit to the archaeological area of the Palatine begins here.

58. *Arch of Titus: panel with the entrance of the procession into the Porta Triumphalis*

59. *Arch of Titus: panel with the triumphal chariot of the emperor*

ANTIQUARIUM FORENSE

In 1900, Giacomo Boni installed the Antiquarium Forense in several rooms adjoining the cloister of S. Maria Nova (usually called S. Francesca Romana), built in the area of the Temple of Venus and Rome. Most of the finds are preserved in a part of the Antiquarium not yet open to the public. Among these, of particular artistic and historical interest are: from the Basilica Fulvia-Aemilia ⑤, the marble frieze of the Caesarean period of which some scenes have been reconstructed (the foundation of the city, the murder of Tarpea, the rape of the Sabines women) and the statues of the barbarian prisoners in pavonazzetto marble; from the *Lacus Iuturnae* ㊵, the archaistic statues of the Dioscures with their horses (second half of the II century B.C.), a II century A.D. copy of the Apollo Philesius of Kanachos, a Greek sculptor of second half of the VI century B.C., the altar with the Dioscures and a large marble *labrum*; from the House of the Vestals ㊼: statues of Numa and three priestesses (II-III century A.D.); from the

Temple of Concord ⑳ in its Tiberian phase: a figurative capital with a pair of rams on the corners; from the Temple of Divus Julius ㉜: fragments of a frieze with archaistic Victories emerging from spirals of acanthus leaves; from the Basilica Julia ㉟: an acroterium with a winged Victory.

The lower floor of the Antiquarium is open to the public. In the entrance, there is a statue in Greek marble of Aesculapius with a child in the act of sacrificing a cock (II century A.D.), excavated in the *Lacus Iuturnae* ㊵. From the cloister, along the walls of which are placed fragments of columns, statues, and architectural decoration, one enters **Room I**, occupied in the centre by a large model of the cemetery excavated by G. Boni between 1902 and 1905 near the Temple of Antoninus and Faustina ㊸, the remains of an even larger

necropolis which must have occupied a vast area of the Forum valley. The glass case along the back wall contains materials from tombs 1-4, excavated around 1950 in the area near the Arch of Augustus ㉞; these tombs represent the earliest evidence for sepulchral use of the Forum valley. They are, in fact, cremation burials containing cinerary urns and miniature funerary equipment dated to the first phase of Latial culture (X century B.C.). The remainder of the exhibition is devoted to the tombs of the cemetery beside the Temple of Antoninus and Faustina ㊸. The earliest tombs belong to phase IIa of Latial culture (900-830 B.C.). The tombs marked with the letters Q, Y, N, A, C, U are "pozzo" tombs with the ash urn (a hut urn or olla) deposited inside a dolium (large vase) of impasto ware containing miniature funerary

60. Statue of Aesculapius from the Lacus Iuturnae

61. Model of the Cemetery near the Temple of Antoninus and Faustina

equipment. All the tombs, with the exception of tomb Q, appear to belong to males. The burial objects in tombs GG, R, S, X, which more than likely refer to females, are of a normal size and include impasto vases and bronze ornaments. The exhibition of the objects within the glass cases presents for each tomb the dolium on the lower shelf, the cinerary urns on the middle shelf and the vases of the funerary equipment on the upper shelf; in correspondence with each tomb, a drawing above the glass case shows a reconstruction of the position of the objects at the time of the excavations. Of particular interest are the hut urns, which document the shape of contemporary houses; foundations of this kind of hut have been excavated on the Palatine. The more or less contemporary inhumation burials indicated by the letters PP, B, KK (cases at the entrance to the room and in the recess behind the model) represent the dead placed on his back on the bottom of more or less rectangular tombs. The materials used for the funerary equipment does not vary significantly from that of the cremation burials. In **Room II**, children's tombs within tree trunks are shown which belong to a later phase of the cemetery (VIII-VII centuries B.C.). Among the burial equipment are notable the more refined pottery and imported or imitation Greek objects. In **Room III** is the material from the area of the Temple of Vesta 46 and in particular from the two wells excavated by A. Bartoli in 1930. Among the objects found in the first well, the oldest and which contains objects dating back to the VII century B.C., noteworthy are the votive vases, the Bucchero ware, the remains of cereals (second shelf), and fragments of impasto tiles and the remains of a grindstone made of volcanic rock (first shelf). The second well was full of objects belonging to the mid and late Republican periods. In addition to the numerous vases of coarse ware or black glaze pottery (third shelf) statuettes, terracotta small altars (arulae) and lamps, spindle-shaped ointment containers, fragments of a flute and bone styluses can be seen. In the centre of the room is a large lead container (cista) with symbols in relief; on the wall is exhibited an inscription with a dedication to Vesta (on the left as we enter). Two cases under the window contain skeletons of a man and a woman found during the excavations carried out in the area of the *Doliola* 29, at one time wrongly identified with the *Equus Domitiani*. The burials contained no funerary equipment but the level to

LE TOMBE A B U V X

62. *Section of Tomb Y with the hut urn and the funerary equipment within the dolium*

63. *Plan and section of Tombs A, B, U, V, X*

64. *Section of Tomb X*

65. *Fragment of black-figure Attic vase with the return of Hephaistos to the Olympus, from the Niger Lapis/Volcanal*

66. *Materials from Tomb Y: among the objects in the funerary equipment is the ritual vase (calefattoio) on the far left*

which they belonged is datable to the VII century B.C. Recently they have been identified as the remains of an expiatory human sacrifice. Leaving Room II, one passes into the last room open to the public, **Room IV**. Here, the glass cases along the walls and in the centre of the room contain the materials belonging to the most ancient phase of the buildings excavated in the Roman Forum. In the glass case dedicated to the *Niger Lapis/Volcanal* ⑥ there are votive objects of Romano-Latial type which testify to a continuity of cult from the second quarter of the VI to the mid I century B.C.: miniature vases of impasto ware, Bucchero ware, Etrusco-Corinthian and Attic pottery (among which the fragments of a black-figure crater from the circle of Lydos, around 560 B.C., representing the return of Hephaistos to the Olympus, (not an unintentional subject considering the place where it was found), bronze statuettes, loom weights, knuckle-bones (astragals), and dice. Material found in the stratigraphy of the Comitium ⑦ follows,

among which of special interest are the fragments of architectural terracottas and of tiles, and from the Cloaca Maxima (in particular the Gnathian and Genucilian pottery). In the other glass cases are objects from the *Regia* ㊺ (styluses, coins, terracotta pots), and a funerary deposit datable to the second quarter of the VII century B.C., found in the *Doliola* ㉙, that is comprised of an olla, a small amphora, two impasto vases, and a one-handled jug of Figulina clay (lower shelf with the old sign that ascribes its provenience to the *Equus Domitiani*). Among the objects from various find spots, noteworthy are a small copy of the Aphrodite of Aphrodisias, integrated with the plaster cast of a fragment preserved in the Vatican Museums, but above all the fragments of the polychrome terracotta decorations found in the lower levels of the Basilica Julia, which perhaps belong to the first phase of decoration of the Temple of the Castores ㊴. The glass

case on the far wall contains above all a collection of Arretine cups and one- or more-handled oil-lamps with triangular or crescent-moon shaped handles. In the case in the centre of the room is displayed the material from the via Sacra and the Republican wells: pottery, statuettes, fragments of a flute (on the side near the window), a saucepan and large bronze weights, a bronze warming-pan with a dedication to Theuda, and terracotta inkpots.

Ch. Hülsen, *Il Foro Romano*, Roma 1905.

E. De Ruggiero, *Il Foro Romano*, Roma 1912.

S.B. Platner,Th. Ashby, *A Topographical Dictionary of Ancient Rome*, Oxford-London 1929.

G. Lugli, *I monumenti antichi di Roma e suburbio*, I-III, Roma 1931-1940.

G. Lugli, *Roma antica. Il centro monumentale*, Roma 1946.

E. Nash, *Pictorial Dictionary of Ancient Rome*, New York 1968².

F. Castagnoli, *Topografia e urbanistica di Roma antica*, Bologna 1969.

P. Zanker, *Il Foro Romano. La sistemazione da Augusto alla tarda antichità*, Roma 1972.

F. Coarelli, *Il Foro Romano, 1. Periodo arcaico*, Roma 1983.

F. Coarelli, *Il Foro Romano, 2. Periodo repubblicano e augusteo*, Roma 1985.

C.F. Giuliani, P. Verduchi, *L'area centrale del Foro Romano*, Firenze 1987.

P. Gros, M. Torelli, *Storia dell'urbanistica. Il mondo romano*, Roma-Bari 1988.

F. Coarelli, *Roma* (Guide archeologiche Laterza), Roma-Bari 1995².

E.M. Steinby (a cura di), *Lexicon Topographicum Urbis Romae*, I-III, Roma 1991-1996 (A-O).

I. Iacopi, *L'Antiquarium Forense* (Itinerari dei musei, gallerie e monumenti d'Italia 112), Roma 1974.

Studies about building and areas in the Roman Forum published in *Lavori e Studi della Soprintendenza Archeologica di Roma* (LSA):

P. Pensabene, *Tempio di Saturno. Architettura e decorazione* (LSA 5); Roma 1984.

Roma. Archeologia nel centro, I. L'area archeologica centrale, (LSA 6,1), Roma 1985.

E. M. Steinby (a cura di), *Lacus Iuturnae* I (LSA 12), Roma 1989.

C. Morselli, E. Tortorici, *Curia, Forum Iulium, Forum Transitorium* (LSA 14,1-14,2), Roma 1989.

I. Nielsen, B. Poulsen et alii (a cura di), *The Temple of Castor and Pollux. The Pre-Augustan Temple Phases with Related Decorative Elements* (LSA 17), Roma 1992.

S. De Angeli, *Templum Divi Vespasiani* (LSA 18), Roma 1992.

Roman Forum plan:
survey by Cooperativa Modus,
Archivio Grafico SAR.

12, 18, 19. from F. Coarelli,
Guida Archeologica di Roma,
Milano 1994², pp. 68, 76, 77.

32. from K. Welch, *The Roman
Arena in late-Republican Italy:
a new interpretation,*
AJA 7, 1994, pp. 69 ss.

3. from H. Broise, J. M. David,
*in Architecture et société de
l'archaïsme grec à la fin de la
Republique romaine,* Actes
Colloque Rome (2-4 dic. 1980),
Roma 1983, pp. 243-45.

6. from *Roma Antiqua.
«Envois» degli architetti francesi
(1788-1924). L'area archeologica
centrale,* Roma 1985, p. 73.

*1, 8, 11, 14, 15, 16, 17, 20, 21,
22, 23, 25, 26, 27, 28, 29, 30,
34, 35, 36, 37, 40, 41, 42, 44,
49, 50, 51, 52, 53, 55, 56, 60.*
Archivio Scala.

*2, 7, 24, 33, 39, 45, 47, 48, 54,
62, 63, 64, 65, 66.*
Archivio Fotografico SAR.

4, 31, 43. from F. Coarelli,
Guida archeologica di Roma,
Milano 1994², pp. 62, 83.

5. from P. Zanker, *Augusto e il
Potere delle immagini,*
Torino 1989, p. 39.

9. Archivio Fotografico
dell'Istituto Archeologico
Germanico.

10, 13, 58, 59, 61.
Archivio Vasari.

38. photo M.A. Tomei.

46. Archivio Anderson.

57. Giovanni Rinaldi,
Il Dagherrotipo.

Illustrations by Ludovico Bisi.

Text: Paola Guidobaldi
Translation by Caterina Guzzo

Reprint 2004
First Edition 1998

© Ministero per i Beni e le Attività Culturali
Soprintendenza archeologica di Roma
An editorial realization by Mondadori Electa S.p.A., Milano

www.electaweb.it

This book was printed for Mondadori Electa S.p.A.
at Mondadori Printing S.p.A., Via Castellana 98, Martellago (Venice)
in the year 2004